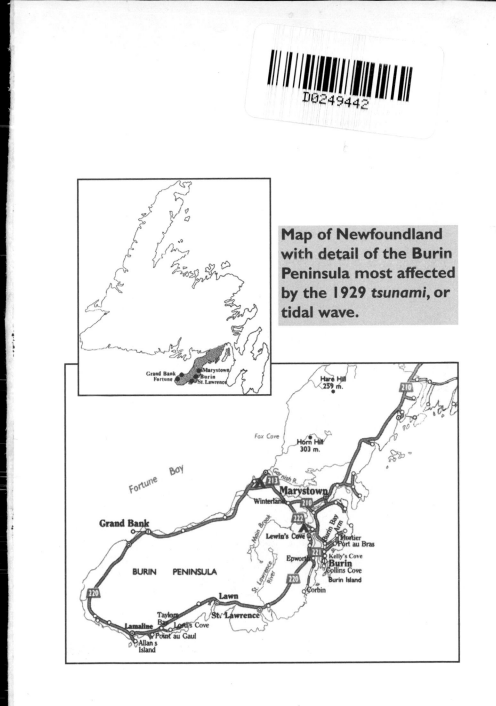

Map of Newfoundland with detail of the Burin Peninsula most affected by the 1929 *tsunami*, or tidal wave.

TSUNAMI

Happy Birthday Dad,

Love,
Kelly
xoxo

TSUNAMI
THE NEWFOUNDLAND
TIDAL WAVE DISASTER

MAURA HANRAHAN

Flanker Press Ltd.
St. John's, NL
2004

Library and Archives Canada Cataloguing in Publication

Hanrahan, Maura, 1963-
    Tsunami: the Newfoundland tidal wave disaster / Maura
Hanrahan.

ISBN 1-894463-63-3

    1. Tsunamis--Newfoundland and Labrador--Burin Peninsula.
2. Burin Peninsula (N.L.)--History--20th century. I. Title.

GC222.B87H35 2004   971.8   C2004-903519-3

Copyright © 2004 by Maura Hanrahan

PRINTED IN CANADA

The publisher wishes to thank Dick Buehler and Paul O'Neill.

First printing Sept. 2004
Second printing Dec. 2004
Third printing Jan. 2005
Fourth printing Jan. 2005

FLANKER PRESS LTD.
P.O. BOX 2522, STATION C
ST. JOHN'S, NL
CANADA
A1C 6K1
TOLL FREE: 1-866-739-4420
TELEPHONE: (709) 739-4477
FAX: (709) 739-4420
INFO@FLANKERPRESS.COM
WWW.FLANKERPRESS.COM

Canada

We acknowledge the financial support of the Government of Canada through the Book
Publishing Industry Development Program (BPIDP) for our publishing program.

For Paul

GLOSSARY

(The) boot: the lower part of the Burin Peninsula

Capstan: a revolving cylinder used to wind an anchor cable

Dory: small, flat-bottomed open fishing boat with pointed bow and stern

Fish and brewis: a traditional Newfoundland meal of boiled fish and
hard tack

Flake: a platform built on poles and spread with boughs for drying fish

Hogshead: a large cask

Lassie bread: bread with molasses on it; a traditional Newfoundland treat

Livyer: permanent settler; people who live in a particular area

Member of the House of Assembly (MHA): elected representative of
the Newfoundland legislature

Old hag: a particularly harrowing form of nightmare; nocturnal terrors
associated with a range of cultural beliefs in Newfoundland

Quintal: a hundredweight (112 lbs.), used as a measure for dried salt cod

(Fishing) room: the waterfront property of a fisherman or merchant,
including the stages, stores, flakes, etc.

Shore fishery: later called the inshore or small boat fishery

Stage: an onshore platform holding working tables and sheds where
women and men processed fish

Store: place where supplies, gear, and dried or salted fish are kept

Token: a vision of an absent friend or relative indicating they will die
within a year

Western boat: a fishing vessel of between fifteen and thirty tons

FOREWORD

In 1929, Newfoundland was a self-governing Dominion, as were Canada, Australia, and other "white" countries within the British Empire. Newfoundland's territory consisted of the seventh largest island in the world, positioned where the Labrador Sea meets the Gulf Stream in the Northwest Atlantic Ocean, and the vast continental land mass of Aboriginal Labrador. The island had been settled by Europeans from the British Isles, the Channel Islands, France, the Iberian Peninsula, and elsewhere for hundreds of years—despite an early British ban on settlement. Some of the settlers married indigenous Mi'kmaq, a few, the Beothuck, members of a small nation that disappeared due to exposure to unfamiliar diseases, loss of access to the seals and fish on the coast, and conflict with those who now encroached on their land.

The settlers and the nations of Europe who sent their fishing fleets were initially attracted by the richest cod fishery in the world. Those who snuck onto the island and dared to over-winter established hundreds of coastal villages where they fished every summer. During the harsh months of November through March they repaired to inland quarters which gave them access to wood and fur-bearing animals.

The island never industrialized in the manner of urbanized countries in Europe and North America; instead, raw materials have always been exported, as they are to this day. This has left Newfoundland relatively cash-poor and sparsely populated but also with fresh air and an enviable slower-paced way of life that persists even into the early twenty-first century.

In 1929, almost thirteen thousand people lived in the seventy-eight communities of the Burin Peninsula, a boot-shaped piece of land that hangs off Newfoundland's South Coast. The peninsula juts out into the North Atlantic as if it is trying to reach the once cod-rich Grand Banks, which have been its life force. Fortune Bay is on one side of the peninsula; Placentia Bay, Newfoundland's largest bay, on the other. For generations the people of the peninsula were engaged in the shore fishery, made up of small boats out of which they fished seasonally, or the Banks fishery, which consisted of schooners that went to the Grand Banks and other offshore locales. They traded their fish to merchants who supplied them with food staples and other goods and a frequently perennial debt burden; this was called the truck system. In turn, their fish went to markets in the West Indies, Spain, Portugal, Italy, Greece, and South America, delivered in Newfoundland schooners. Thus, some Burin Peninsula fishermen were among the most well travelled people in the world. They brought back oranges and bananas for their children, silk and satin for their wives, Jamaican rum for themselves, as well as rich stories to fire everyone's imaginations.

At first, the 1929 October Bank Crash, which signalled the beginning of the Great Depression, seemed not to mean much to the rural people of the Burin Peninsula. Later, when fish prices dropped dramatically, its effects would become startlingly clear to them and to Newfoundlanders in general, as they would to people all over the western world.

Even now, though, the people of the Burin Peninsula remember 1929 for the tidal wave, the great *tsunami* caused by an underwater earthquake that struck their shores. The ruptures from the deep that night measured 7.2 on the Richter scale and caused the sea floor to move several yards. The subterranean quake forced waves across the ocean at speeds of more than eight hundred kilometres an hour. Most *tsunamis* develop in the Ring of Fire, the region that encircles the Pacific Ocean. Although tidal waves (as they are commonly but mistakenly called in this part of the world) are not unknown in Newfoundland, the island is obviously far away from the Ring of Fire. Thus, the *tsunami* that hit the Burin Peninsula came as a complete shock to the people who lived there. This book tells their story.

PART ONE: WAVES

1

It would be carved into the children's store of memories for-ever. In Lawn, on the boot of the Burin Peninsula, as the evening of Monday, November 18 drew in, six-year-old Anna Tarrant lay on a day bed in her family's kitchen, suffering from a sore throat. It was the time of year for colds, the child's mother had said that morning. Anna, wearing a white flannel night-gown, amused herself by playing cat's cradle. She snuggled into the thick cotton quilt her mother had covered her with to keep off the chill.

Suddenly the odd sound of dishes rattling caught Anna's attention. Her eyes scanned the kitchen counters and cupboards, but she could see nothing. The eerie sound continued. Then, still beneath the quilt, Anna looked for the Tarrants' old tabby. Had he bumped into some dishes?

Anna called to her mother who had just come into the room with some blue potatoes and thick round carrots from the root cellar. Mrs. Tarrant was harried. She blew a strand of dark brown hair off her face as she rushed into the kitchen.

"Mommy, where's the cat?" Anna said.

"Here, Anna," came the reply. "Right behind me."

Out from Mrs. Tarrant's skirts came the family pet—straight from the root cellar.

On the day bed Anna filled with fright.

Twelve-year-old Mary Kehoe of Red Head Cove in Conception Bay North was aboard the SS *Nerissa* with her father, Martin, bound for New York. Once the ship left St. John's, she was in rough seas. The decks were cleared and below, passengers bit their nails in fear. Others clutched their hands to their hearts and emptied the contents of their bellies. Mary's father lay next to her in her bunk, holding his daughter tight so she wouldn't be thrown onto the cabin deck. To make matters worse, Mary's stomach churned with seasickness.

Back home in Red Head Cove, Mary's brother and sisters marvelled at the sight of pots and pans dancing around on the stove. It was as if the household items had decided to put on a performance for them. Then the children's eyes looked up in unison at the ceiling while the house shook.

"It's a real windy night!" the littlest sister said.

"No, it's more than that," her brother answered solemnly.

Meanwhile, as the *Nerissa* slowly made her way along the Southern Shore past Ferryland light and Chance Cove, Mary and her father, Martin Kehoe, raised quiet prayers to the heavens for their safe passage.

*

Five-year-old Aubrey King stood with his horse in the garden of his home in Point au Gaul, a village on the bottom of the Burin Peninsula. In the last moments of the afternoon, young Aubrey fed the horse hay and tried to push some into its mouth, like a mother feeds a baby. The boy patted the animal's dark snout. "Atta boy," he murmured. Then, as he had done so many times before, he stepped back to admire the animal's large body; his appreciative eyes took in its sleekness, strength, and bulk. The horse was a work animal, part of the machinery that kept the family economy going through the year; it was used to haul wood in the winter and do farmwork in the summer. But little Aubrey loved it like a pet and the animal responded in kind.

Then, late in the afternoon when dusk was nothing more than a hint, Aubrey's horse suddenly bit him. The boy drew back, ashen-faced and breathless. Then the ground beneath the two of them quivered and shook. The horse grew skittish and Aubrey, still reeling from the shock of the bite, was too afraid to comfort him.

He ran into the house, even as the earth continued to shake under his feet. There he was greeted by the sight of his mother frozen in front of a picture of her father that had fallen from the wall for no reason at all.

In Great Burin, well to the north of Point au Gaul, eleven-year-old Sam Adams was outside in his family's garden when, late in the afternoon, he felt a tremor under his feet. It was a strange sensation but it didn't last any time at all and it was mild.

"Did you feel that?" Sam called out to a neighbour.

"Yes, like the earth moved a little," his friend answered.

Sam nodded. "What do you suppose it was?" he asked. The other boy shook his head and shrugged. Sam dismissed the tremor as one of the mysteries of life, like stars falling to the earth or whales beaching themselves. He left the garden and went inside, where his mother told him that some dishes stored in the cupboard had shook so much she feared they might break. Sam told his mother about the tremor but the two of them did not know what to make of it.

Bessie Hennebury of Lord's Cove, not far from Point au Gaul, was almost fifteen in November, 1929. She was in her father's fishing room, helping to weigh his dried fish so it could be collected and shipped away to market. She was standing by the big weights that Mike Harnett, the merchant's agent, had brought with him to weigh the fish. As she passed the fish to Harnett, everything started shaking: the fish, the tables, the walls, the weights. Indeed, it seemed as if the very ground under them was moving. The clanging sound of the metal weights seemed like it would not stop. It scared Bessie so much that she bolted out of the fishing room, running straight home. She raced up the hill, away from the beach and the water, her heart pummelling her chest walls so that she thought it would break them open. She did not look behind her to see what was happening. As she ran, she didn't notice if the earth beneath her was shaking here, too; she was desperate to think the tremor was restricted to the fishing rooms.

In Burin Bay Arm, George and Ernest Pike, brothers of ten and eight, were in a hillside meadow above their home. The afternoon was so windless that the meadow grass was motionless. Running through the late fall air was a thread of coolness that hinted at the winter that was just around the corner. Above the boys, though, the skies were an azure blue and cloudless. The Atlantic far below was quiet as if asleep.

The weather was of no concern to the Pike brothers, though. The boys had one thing in mind: their neighbour Mrs. Moulton's sheep. Mrs. Moulton kept sheep to make wool to sell for a bit of cash, and to have some mutton once in awhile. Some of the old lady's sheep had somehow escaped from the meadow and Mrs. Moulton was distraught. She was offering twenty-five cents to anyone who could return the strays. The Pike boys were delighted at the opportunity to make a little cash. They had spent their dinner break and the walk home from school planning how they would retrieve the lost sheep. Now, George and Ernest bent over a hole in the fence that surrounded the meadow, intent on their task as they attached a rope snare in the hopes of catching a sheep. In their minds' eyes were the hard candies they would buy and savour if their venture was successful.

It wasn't long before they were rewarded. But as soon as a sheep was caught in the snare, the boys were startled by the arrival of a motor car, one of the few in the area. The car turned around just below the meadow. George and Ernest fell to the hard ground on their bellies, trying to hide from the car's occupants; they thought the people in the car might think they were doing something wrong by catching the sheep.

Then without warning, the ground shook with great force.

"What's that?" George asked.

"The car must have her winter chains on," Ernest answered.

"You're crazy," his brother replied. "Chains on a car wouldn't shake the ground like that."

Ernest frowned. He didn't know what was going on. When the car left the area, the shaking and the bold noise that accompanied stopped. George and Ernest rose and smoothed out their jackets and pants.

"I don't know what that was," George said, staring out at the ocean as if it held the answer. Ernest looked at him, expecting him to say more, but he didn't.

Then the two boys turned their attention back to the task at hand. They took the sheep out of the rope snare and led it out of the meadow and down to Mrs. Moulton's. The old lady was standing outside her house, wearing a white cotton apron and a winter coat that she had evidently thrown over her shoulders. She was surrounded by her family, some of whom were pacing back and forth on the road.

"Look at that commotion!" George said.

"I'm not going back in for the money!" one of Mrs. Moulton's sons cried. From their talk, the Pike boys realized the Moultons were convinced the house was haunted. They thought there was a ghost under the house, a ghost who had caused the stove covers to jump, the dishes to rattle and break, and the pictures to fall off the wall. As they fretted over the ghost shifting the house as it had, Ernest realized they thought the tremor was specific to their house. He knew then it had been more general, taking in at least part of the village all the way to the meadow and possibly beyond. He thought of telling the Moultons this but they were too panicked to listen to him, he figured. And in spite of everything that was happening, the succulent candy remained uppermost in Ernest's mind. It was getting late, his mother would expect the boys to return home soon, so he decided to take care of business.

He stepped forward to announce their success in catching Mrs. Moulton's sheep. When her son reached for it, he shook his head.

"No money, no sheep," he said.

The Moultons stopped talking and the men looked at each other. Mrs. Moulton poked one of them. "I want my sheep back," she said.

Her son sighed and went into the house, walking slowly as he did. He came out with twenty-five cents and handed it to Ernest. The boys pocketed their reward and went home.

At Lawn, where Anna Tarrant struggled with her sore throat, a bevy of school boys avoided their homework by playing soccer before supper. They were soccer mad in Lawn and in the villages adjacent to it. They started playing the game not long after they could walk.

One of the smaller boys who played that afternoon, Austin Murphy, was just seven. In the middle of the game he stopped to take a rest. He sat on a flat grey rock on the side of the meadow that served as their soccer pitch and took in the unusual brightness of the late fall day. He could see the bay from where he was and, beyond that, the wide Atlantic Ocean, which was as smooth as a baby's bottom for once. It put Austin in mind of mid-summer, though the nip in the air reminded him it was nearly winter.

Suddenly, the rock shook under him for a full three or four seconds. At first he looked down at it between his skinny little legs, noticing the shaking grass that surrounded it. After the first second or two, he turned his eyes to the boys still playing soccer. They had stopped. They were looking around, too, just as he was.

13

It wasn't just this rock, then; it was the whole place that was shaking. Perhaps all of Lawn was quaking—or maybe even the whole of Newfoundland.

Austin sat there wondering what was going on. His mates gathered to him. They, too, were flummoxed.

"I never saw anything like that before," said one of the team captains.

"It was something strange all right," one of the boys agreed.

None of them were scared; it just hadn't occurred to them to be afraid, especially since nothing came after the initial tremor.

Then one of the older boys came up with an answer that satisfied them all.

"I know just what it was," he announced, spinning the soccer ball on his forefinger. "It's the engines starting up in the powerhouse. That's what made that shaking."

The boys nodded. The United Towns Electric Company had all but completed the installation of a hydro-electric plant on Northeast River near Lawn. In November, 1929 the company was about to put the plant into operation, as everyone knew. However, the generators would be turned by water-driven turbines which would make a scarcely audible humming sound. The boys on the soccer pitch, of course, could not know this. They had no way to know that what they had witnessed was the beginning of a *tsunami*.

2

Sarah Ann Rennie bent over her Singer sewing machine. She wanted to get a start on her sewing before it got too dark. She hated sewing under the lamp and having to squint; she wanted to save her eyes. She had cut up a shirt of Martin's, her oldest, and was making it into two shirts for Bernard, the baby. She smiled at her own ingenuity. She knew her long dead mother would be pleased. Her fingers moved in unison, pushing the blue cotton under the needle, as her right foot worked the pedal.

On the black pot-bellied stove was a huge steel pot full of potatoes, carrots, and turnips from Sarah's root cellar. Sarah had them on slow boil. She'd round out the meal with a bit of salt fish and some of the bread she made every day. She might even let the children have some molasses, though, like all the women in Lord's Cove and the rest of the communities on the coast, she had to spare it along through the winter.

Sarah was a Fitzpatrick before she married Patrick Rennie of nearby Lamaline. She was born in Lord's Cove in 1892 and baptized seven weeks later when they could get handy to the priest at Allan's Island, right by Lamaline. Her father still lived next door to her in Lord's Cove, alongside The Pond on the eastern side of the cove. The children came right away: Martin, Albert, Rita, Patrick, named for his father, Margaret, and Bernard. There would probably be more, Sarah knew, and when she thought of this, she smiled.

She glanced at baby Bernard as she sewed. At eighteen months, his cheeks were round and pink, the picture of health. He was lively and Sarah had tied him into his high chair. Blond curls framed his face and he called out as he banged his rattle on his high chair table. He was already a handful, this child, Sarah thought, laughing at him as she took a scissors to the cloth in her hands.

Nine-year-old Rita and seven-year-old Patrick played with a spinning top in the pantry. Their little sister, Margaret, only four, was in there with them. Sarah could hear the whir of the top and then the thud as it hit the floor. Then she heard the scuff of Rita's and Patrick's shoes on the plank floor. They might be playing school now or house, she thought, alongside the barrels of herring, mackerel, and cod that stood against the pantry wall. Above them hung a brace of rabbits and a row of jars, filled with pickled onions and beets. There were jam jars there, too, containing blueberries and strawberries. Sarah even had some rhubarb jam left, though her children loved it and it was November. Patrick and his sisters were particularly close, little mates, their mother called them. Sarah let them idle with their games before supper and their lessons. They'd have a long dark winter ahead of them and all that trekking to school in the cold, poor mites. And Rita was getting old enough to be a real help to her. She'd let them play when they could.

When the tremor came, Sarah was too face-and-eyes into her sewing machine to notice it. Her foot pushed heavily on the pedal as the needle dove into the pieces of cotton, tying them together. The clack-clack of the machine quickened as she worked and the earth trembled. In the pantry, Rita and Patrick stopped their play as the quake began and laughed at the tremor.

Across the harbour in Lord's Cove, a group of fishermen played cards at Prosper Walsh's. They were glad for the leisure. They had spent every waking hour from June until September on the water or bringing their fish in to the beaches for the women to cure. At sea they went to the same grounds their fathers and grandfathers fished. They caught squid and slammed it onto the dozens of hooks on the lines they let out into the water. When they hauled the lines in, they tore codfish off the hooks and threw them into the bellies of their dories. Some days the men roasted in the sun; other days the fog drifted up from the St. Pierre Bank and seeped into their bones. Their wrists constantly itched and pained with the salt water blisters they called water pups. Their backs ached from the bending over; their hands and fingers grew red with nicks and cuts. At night they flopped on their beds, dead weights. During the fall and winter they hunted partridge and snared rabbits, cut wood, and repaired their fishing gear, making new nets and trawls. But, unlike the summer, in fall and winter there was time for a Christmas dance, some mummering, and the odd game of cards with friends.

Patrick Rennie, Sarah's husband, laughed out loud when he won a hand. "Look Martin! Look Albert!" he called to his oldest sons. "Your father's won!" He might have been awarded the crown jewels for the smile on his face, russet with years of fishing. The boys smiled, delighted to be among the men. Martin, just into his teens, had been on the water all summer with his father and had not returned to school; he was a man now, a fisherman. Albert intended to follow him.

They were starting to run low on rum and someone mentioned that there was none left in the village.

"Never mind," one of the card players said. "A few of the fellows have gone over to St. Pierre. I daresay that's what their errand was for. They should be back this evening. And they might have a drink for us!"

The men sat around the Walshs' kitchen table while the boys stood behind them, peeking at their cards. Half empty cups of tea stood on the table, as did a few glasses of rum. Suddenly the table shook and the cups and glasses did a little jig. Patrick was the first to laugh, triggering a similar reaction in most of his friends. His sons giggled as well.

But then Prosper Walsh spoke up.

"That was no laughing matter," he said. His dark eyes fixed on each man and boy, one by one. "Hear what I'm saying. That was an earthquake. And there's going to be a tidal wave next."

"Go 'way with you, Prosper," one of the men said as he shuffled the deck of cards.

But Prosper shook his head. He had been on schooner crews and had travelled to places these shore fishermen had never been: the Caribbean, the Mediterranean, North Africa. He had been in earthquakes, seen tidal waves, lived through the eyes of southern hurricanes.

"No, fellows," he said. "It's no joke. I'm telling you there's going to be a tidal wave. Look—there's going to be a big storm, here onshore."

"Have another drink, Prosper," one of the fishermen said, bringing gales of laughter from the others.

"We've got to get all the women and children to dry land," Prosper pleaded. "It won't be safe right down in the village."

"Are you going to build an ark, too?" the same fisherman asked.

"God help us if I'm right," said Prosper. "This whole place will be swamped by a great big sea while you fellows play cards."

As Prosper spoke, young Martin Rennie found he couldn't laugh with the rest of the boys and men, even as his father and brother did. In his chest was a monkey's fist that kept twisting tighter and tighter. By the end of the conversation he was as stiff as a cold junk with fear.

Lord's Cove lies at the tip of the Burin Peninsula and is shaped like a horseshoe, with high hills rising way up out of the sea ringing the harbour. Lord's Cove is likely named after the rainbow-feathered Harlequin ducks that frequent its shores and were nicknamed lords and ladies by the island's early settlers.

One family was living in Lord's Cove by 1800, at least for the duration of the summer, to fish; they might have repaired to the less exposed woods for the winter, as most early rural Newfoundlanders did. They had no doctor or nurse, just their own common sense and the kitchen medicine their mothers bred into their bones. By the middle of the century, the fifty fishermen of Lord's Cove had nineteen boats from which they caught more than five hundred quintals of codfish as well as four barrels of salmon, worth more than five hundred pounds. They had cattle, milch cows, and sheep as insurance against hunger. They also had eighty-five acres of land under cultivation. Ten years later their children were taking lessons, in a house, not a school—it would be another half century before they'd have one.

By 1921, eight years before the earth rumbled for a full five minutes on a beautiful November evening, there were 208 people living in Lord's Cove. In its harbour were forty-six boats and seventeen fishing rooms. They had built a community.

Unlike nearby Point May and Taylor's Bay, Lord's Cove wasn't built on flat land and surrounded by meadows and semi-tundra with the woods way in behind. Here the trees came almost right up to the village, combining with the hills and jumble of two-storey clapboard houses to make for a cozy feeling. The rich cod fishing grounds were just offshore, too, giving the men of Lord's Cove an advantage that their brethren in more sheltered parts of Placentia Bay and elsewhere in Newfoundland lacked.

An hour or more had passed and Prosper Walsh had abandoned his friends at their card game as his heart ached at their indifference to his warning. Young Martin Rennie followed him out the door, casting a backward glance at his father, Patrick, and brother, Albert, still enjoying the game. Prosper ignored the boy at his heels and banged on his neighbour's door, calling out, "We're going to have a tidal wave! Get to higher ground."

Bruised from his experience with the card players, he didn't wait to gauge anyone's reaction this time. Instead, he went from one house to another as if in a barn dance, calling as loudly as he could, "We're going to have a tidal wave! Get to higher ground."

Martin saw two women standing in the pathway between their houses, looking after Prosper as he sped along banging on doors.

"I believe him," said one. "I'm getting my youngsters and going up to the woods."

"My husband is not back yet from the cards," her friend responded, shaking her head. "He's not worried. Why should I be?"

"I'm not waiting for my husband," came the reply. "I'm the captain of the shore crew anyway."

Martin was glued to the ground but he willed his feet to move. He didn't follow Prosper this time. He headed back to the Walsh's kitchen; he would try and convince his father and brother that Prosper was right and that they must act quickly to get their mother Sarah and the little children to the safety of the woods.

3

To the south, Nan and Herbert Hillier were walking to Lamaline from their home in Point au Gaul for an Orange Lodge meeting scheduled for seven o'clock that evening. Nan had spent the day baking blueberry pies and sponge cakes for the gathering. She had picked the blueberries that fall with the help of her two eldest, Leslie, ten, and Ruby, eight; the berries had been the fruit of a bumper crop. Ruby had helped her with the sponge cakes, too. Then Nan and her husband packed the baked goods in a suitcase for the three mile journey. It was a beautiful evening; with the sun about to go down in a cloudless sky, the autumn air was bracing, just the way Nan liked it. There was no wind and hence, almost no noise from the sea, something they were not used to.

At about the halfway point between Point au Gaul and Lamaline, the earth began to tremble and Nan and Herbert froze in their boots. Nan looked up to see telegraph wires vibrating and emitting a loud buzz, as if they might explode. She drew toward Herbert, too shocked to speak. She tried to steady her feet on the hard ground but the rumbling of the earth continued a full minute. Then it stopped.

When it was over she cried, "Herbert, what's happening?"

Her husband, a veteran of the first world war, had been to southern climes and recognized what he had just witnessed. "It's an earth tremor, Nan," he said gently.

"Will we go back home?" Nan asked anxiously, thinking of their children. Besides Leslie and Ruby, she had two little boys, Lawson and Charlie. She wondered if they had felt the tremor too, and were frightened. She assumed it went all the way to Point au Gaul, seeing as it travelled on the telegraph wires like that.

Herbert stomped his feet as if to demonstrate the steadiness of the earth. He smiled broadly. "Solid again!" he said. "No, it's nothing. We'll go on."

Nan, in her shyness, always deferred to Herbert. She looked around, trying to convince herself that everything had returned to normal. She relaxed and breathed in the comfort of the clean air.

They crossed the three-hundred-foot-long Salmonier Bridge, bringing them into the next community. In Lamaline everyone was talking about the rumbling; it seemed that no one had experienced such a thing before. Some of the women told Nan their houses had shaken as if they would never stop. They had run outside in fright and been too afraid to go back into their homes. When it was over, they finally went inside to find dishes and glassware scattered and broken all over their kitchen floors. Although the earth seemed to have returned to its usual quietude, they were still frightened. When Herbert registered the women's fear, he came over and explained the nature of earth tremors to them. Then he added, "It's over and finished."

But, try as she might, Nan could not stop thinking of her children back in Point au Gaul.

Point au Gaul lies at the bottom of the Burin Peninsula, flat and exposed to the North Atlantic Ocean, not far from St. Pierre Bank and north of the famous Grand Banks that had been a food basket for numerous nations for centuries. At Point au Gaul a narrow beach runs for half a mile, separating the cold waves from the level grasslands that reach far inland to the low-lying coniferous woods. The name Point au Gaul may be a translation of Frenchman's Point, a reference to the first European settler, a man from France called Hillier. The area was of vital importance to French fishermen for many years; they recognized its easy access to abundant cod stocks and the usefulness of its flat land and beaches for drying fish.

The settlers of Point au Gaul had strong connections to the nearby French island of St. Pierre, where they traded their surplus vegetables and sometimes met the man or woman they would marry. Over the years, French families moved into the village—the Martins, Millons, and Roberes among them. With one eye on the lucrative fishery in the area, a merchant set up shop around the turn of the century.

In 1921, the village's fifty-eight fishermen along with thirty-eight women working on the beach had produced fish products worth $13,328—a considerable sum. By November, 1929, Point au Gaul was a vigorous community of well over two hundred people, a good size outport for this part of the Burin Peninsula. Most of the forty-five houses straddled the grasses that bordered the narrow beach in Point au Gaul. They were, then, very close to the waves of the North Atlantic. For them, this represented riches, not danger.

Back home in Point au Gaul that crisp November evening, the tremor was all the talk as well. No one understood what was going on. Twelve-year-old Caroline Hillier, a very distant relative of Nan's, felt the hairs on her head stiffen as the rumbling seemed to go on and on. She had been in her family's house, helping in the kitchen. Like many in the village, Caroline had run outside with her mother and her toddler brother, Ben, to see what was happening and to get away from the weird sound of dishes rattling. But there was no way to escape the thunder that accompanied the shaking. Caroline bit her lip as she listened to the older people talk of the mystery and her breathing grew rapid and shallow. She clutched her mother's hand and touched little Ben's stockinged foot, dangling as his mother held him. The human contact reassured her and she calmed slightly, but the terrible shaking of the ground below them continued. And then, just as suddenly as it had come, it halted.

"Thank God!" someone called out.

"It's not the end of the world, then," said another neighbour in relief.

"Not yet anyway," another weighed in, trying to sound light-hearted.

They looked at the sky, as if they hoped the face of God might appear to tell them not to worry. But there was nothing in the sky, not a single fluffy cloud, not a single black-backed gull or sooty shearwater. The air was crisp and clear and a windless graveyard stillness descended upon the village and the rest of the coast. Though their hearts still fluttered in their chests, it was impossible to believe that anything untoward could happen now. And clearly "the Big Thump," as the people of Point au Gaul had already begun to call it, was over.

Still jumpy, Caroline scanned the village with her eyes. It was then that she saw Joe Miller, an old man from France who had moved to Point au Gaul. He seems to be up to something, Caroline thought from her station on an incline known as "Up the Hill." Joe Miller was on the level ground that adjoined the beach and the fishing rooms known as "Down the Town." He was on his knees. Caroline let go of her mother's hand and Ben's little foot and rushed Down the Town. She shimmied her way into the small crowd that had by now gathered around old Joe. She saw that his ear was pressed to the ground and his eyes were closed. The group watched him in silence as dusk drew in on this strangest of nights. He remained in his position for several minutes.

Finally, Joe hauled himself up and stood. He folded his arms in front of his chest and announced, "Prepare yourselves for a tidal wave."

"What?"

"Prepare yourselves for a tidal wave," he repeated in his thick French accent.

"A tidal wave indeed," one man said. "Joe, it's a perfectly calm evening."

Joe pursed his lips but said nothing. Caroline stared at him. The little crowd murmured among themselves. How could there be any kind of storm on an evening like this? She saw Joe shrug as the crowd began to disperse.

Caroline was inclined to agree with them. She was getting fed up with all this rumbling and dire talk. She wanted to get back to her own house. Her father's birthday, the twenty-first of November, was in a few days and they were having a party! Caroline could never remember her father celebrating his birthday before, which only added to the excitement.

"Yes, child, this is the first one he's ever marked," her mother had said to her as they added raisins to the fruitcake they were making. They'd have a sponge cake but he loved fruitcake so they were making that as well. He could take it with him when he went on his next work trip. The idea for the celebration came from Thomas, Caroline's father. One quiet black night in late August, he told his wife, "I feel the need to visit with my close friends, with my buddies. I want to have a little celebration with them."

His wife, Lydia, nodded, though she frowned a little at her husband's circumspect tone. She had never heard him talk in this manner before; he sounded like an old man.

"My birthday is a good time to do it," he said.

"It is," Lydia smiled. "It's a grand time."

Thomas Hillier was a fish oil inspector for the government of Newfoundland. Fish oil was an important export and Hillier's work required him to travel all over the country, ensuring that outgoing products were of high quality. Caroline often missed him when he was gone; so did Lydia, a native of Grand Bank who had moved to Point au Gaul upon her marriage and was now expecting another child in a couple of months.

Besides her little brother, Ben, Caroline had two older half-siblings, Harold, nineteen, and Georgina, twenty, children from her father's first marriage, making for a full household. Like Nan Hillier who fretted for her children back home, Harold and Georgina had gone to the Orange Lodge supper meeting in Lamaline. The Hillier siblings walked to Lamaline with their friends, David and Jessie Hipditch, the parents of three small children who they'd left in the care of Jessie's parents back in Point au Gaul. When Jessie Hipditch felt the tremor, she saw her eight month old daughter Elizabeth in front of her face, waving at her. Then the child disappeared. It was the oddest sensation, but it was hard to pay it any mind with the blue skies and the windless air.

4

Five-year-old Pearl Brushett yawned as she sat on the edge of her bed. She slowly pulled her socks off, forgetfully throwing them on the floor. When the left one gently flopped on the soft-wood, she threw herself back on her bed and sighed gratefully. She wasn't used to school, this was her first year, and it was tiring her out. It was a long walk to the schoolhouse, she had to struggle to keep up with her big brother, Fred, who was ten. And it seemed so long until dinner every day. In the classroom she often found herself staring out the window thinking of her doll, Annie, and wishing she was home, tucking Annie in and telling her a story.

"Miss Brushett!" the teacher called those times. Pearl could never relax. That was what was wearing her out.

She remembered her sock on the floor. She rose from the bed, then leaned down and picked it up, taking the other in her hand as well. She carried them to the brin bag her mother kept in a closet in the hallway. It was full of dirty clothes, it always was;

there were seven of them in the Brushett family and it seemed Carrie, Pearl's mother, could never get to the bottom of the brin bag no matter how hard she tried.

Pearl smoothed her flannelette nightie and pulled back her bed clothes. She puffed up her pillow, turned around, and sank onto her bed. Her seven-year-old sister, Lillian, already lay in bed, white-faced with an earache. Their mother, Carrie, had warmed up a plate and wrapped it in a blanket; Lillian lay with it under her head now trying to derive some comfort from it. Poor Lillian, Pearl thought, as she shimmied into bed. Pearl's other sister, Lottie, who was eight, would be in soon, too. Between the two of them, the bed would be all warmed up for her.

"Mommy!" she called. She could not go to sleep without her mother's good night kiss.

"I'll be there in a minute," Carrie answered. "I'm just tucking in your little brother."

Pearl was already floating toward sleep when she felt her mother's soft lips on her forehead.

"You're my good girl, aren't you?" Carrie said softly.

Pearl nodded sleepily, smiling. How she loved the sound of her mother's voice.

"Here, make sure Annie is tucked in there with you," Carrie said, pulling the covers tight around her daughter. "Good night now. Sweet dreams always."

"Always," Pearl whispered.

Pearl's home was in Kelly's Cove on Great Burin Island, the site of two other villages, Shalloway, and Great Burin. With other settlements on the peninsula nearby, including Whale Cove, Kirby's

Cove, Burin Bay, Collin's Cove, Ship Cove, and Path End, Kelly's Cove was part of Burin. A rocky area of sheltered coves, Burin may be named for an engraving tool, *burine* in French; according to legend, a French sailor was on deck holding a *burine* when he noticed how it resembled the harbour.

The European presence here came early. Basque fishermen frequented *Buria Audia* (Great Burin) and *Buria Chumea* (Little Burin) as early as 1650. In 1662, the parliament of Brittany, France, allotted forty fishermen to Great Burin. The English did not come until 1718, when Christopher Spurrier of Poole, England, established his shipbuilding enterprise at Ship Cove (thus giving it its name presumably). By 1740, 130 English men, women, and children over-wintered, becoming the first permanent European settlers. They were later joined by substantial numbers of Jersey fishermen. Burin received imports of salt meat, rum, molasses, and salt, and became the capital of the bay.

Like most of the men on Great Burin Island, Pearl's father, William, was a fisherman. William was in the shore fishery and had a good season in 1929. He'd had several good years, in fact, as had most of his neighbours. The people of Burin knew about the Bank Crash in New York and the Depression that was beginning to sink economies all over the western world but they were not too worried about themselves. They had put a bit away during their good years. They had learned to be prudent over the years, to take absolutely nothing for granted. William Brushett was out of debt now and he intended to stay that way. When he talked about the Bank Crash with his neighbours they spoke of their pity for urban dwellers.

"At least we got our pantries full of food," William would say. "Salt cod, herring, a bit of salmon and smoked caplin. Root crops. Things we can hunt. We'll never starve to death, but I don't know what will happen to those people in the cities with this Bank Crash and the money worth nothing."

William had thought of these things as he walked into the woods on the fine, clear morning of November 18, 1929, his axe in his hand. He drank in the cool autumn air and enjoyed the sounds of chickadees and juncos. He took long strides, his belly contented with the scrambled eggs and bacon Carrie had prepared for his breakfast. The tea she made, too, it was always wonderful; somehow, she always made the best tea.

William was on his way to get the family's winter supply of wood. He'd gone in the bay, away from rocky Burin, and later when the snow came, he would bring his horse back to fetch his cords of wood. It was a beautiful day for a journey of any kind and he imagined that Carrie would have made good use of the kind weather to wash and dry clothes. You almost couldn't believe winter was at hand.

Someone was shaking Pearl. Was it that strange rumbling again? She hoped not; she hadn't liked that at all. She just wanted to sleep. But her mother wouldn't let her.

"Wake them up, Mommy!" she thought she heard Lottie say.

"Pearl, get up," Carrie said. Pearl heard the firmness in her voice.

"Mommy, I'm tired," Pearl mumbled. "I'm too tired to go to school."

"Pearl, get up now," Carried insisted. Pearl sat up in bed at once. "Get up and put this on."

it right: "If you have [a business you think could work, do it on a scale and see," says Marissa Shipman.

Her mother tossed her winter coat at her. Pearl rubbed her eyes. She was surprised to see her older brother, Fred, standing in her room, all dressed in his winter clothes. Her mother held little James, also wearing his winter coat. The bed was empty beside her, and Lottie was standing next to their brothers shivering. The room was dark; it must be night still, Pearl thought. What was going on?

The little girl jumped out of bed and wrapped her winter coat around her. She stared at her mother who was peeping out through the curtains which she had drawn tightly together. Pearl leaned over to look, but Carrie tightened the curtains in her hand.

"Keep away from the window!" she ordered.

But Pearl had already seen crushed stages and flakes and the debris-filled harbour. But she knew it wasn't Kelly's Cove.

"Mommy, what's happening?" she asked. She looked at her mother whose face was tight in a frown. Carrie said nothing. Pearl looked at her brother Fred. As he opened his mouth, he caught his mother's eye and clamped shut. Pearl raised huge eyes to her mother's face. Then she noticed that the floor underneath her seemed unsteady.

"Hold onto the bedpost, children!" Carrie said. The baby in her arms began to wail. Carrie's knuckles went white as she continued to peer out through the sliver of an opening in the curtains.

Then the house seemed as if it were flying. The older children clung to the bedpost even as the bed slid across the floor. Carrie clutched James and stood with her back flat against the wall at a right angle to the window. Somehow she stayed upright.

"Mommy!" the children cried in unison.

Then the house stopped flying and everything seemed to stop.

"It's still," Pearl cried. "Mommy, where are we?"

Carrie drew back the curtain slightly and let out a great gasp. "Oh God, my God, thank God" she said. "We're back home."

She laid the baby and her toddler on Pearl's bed and picked up her daughter's chair. She hurled it through the window.

"Help!" she cried. "Help us!"

Pearl's mouth hung open as blood ran down her mother's wrist but Carrie ignored it. Then she rushed to the window and watched her chair fly to the ground. My father built that chair, she thought, pout-faced.

"Help us!" her mother cried again.

"We can go downstairs," said Pearl's brother Fred. "We can get out that way."

"Good boy," said Carrie. "See if you can do that."

The boy left Pearl's bedroom and hurried down the narrow hallway to the stairs. But he stopped at the top; the stairway was covered in frigid seawater. Below him chairs, table legs, and his mother's knitting floated eerily. He screamed.

"Mommy! We can't go down there!" he howled. "The stairs are full of water."

"It's all right, it's all right," Carrie said, though her breathing came rapidly. "Ben and Beatrice Hollett are down there. See? They see us. They're going to get us." She took her son's hand and led him toward the broken window.

Pearl was shivering now. But she couldn't stop thinking about her broken chair. She still didn't know what had happened. How could the stairs be full of water? Was she dreaming? Perhaps she was being visited by the old hag? None of this made any sense...

34

With little James perched on her hip, Carrie ran back to the top of the stairs. She exhaled in relief when she saw that the water was low enough that they could walk downstairs.

"Come on, children!" she cried. "Everyone follow me."

Fred, Lottie, Lillian who had retrieved her still warm plate for her ear, and Pearl trailed after their mother down the stairs through icy water. They let out shrieks as the coldness pierced their bones. They looked from the sea water to the parlour window as they heard the shattering of glass.

Then Pearl felt her mother's arms around her and she was being passed to someone on a ladder. He carried her to the beach. It was freezing. Her little brother James was crying. Her mother was still in the house with her big brother. "We went all the way to Bartlett's Island!" Carrie cried. Really? Pearl wondered. Then they were all on the beach. She blanched at the crimson that was spreading across her mother's arm.

"She needs a bandage," Beatrice Hollett said.

"Get to higher ground!" someone called. Maybe it was Mr. Hollett. They ran as fast as they could to Humpess Head, Pearl holding Carrie's hand. Something was chasing them. As they ran, Pearl glanced behind to see that it was a wall of ice water and it took their house again and carried it away where they could no longer see it. On the hill where they finally found safety, Carrie Brushett pulled her five children to her and sobbed from the deepest part of her belly.

When William Brushett rowed into Kelly's Cove on Great Burin Island two days later, his heart was thumping. He had felt the rumbling, heard the thunder, and watched the walls of water steal houses and take lives. The night before he reached Kelly's Cove he paced a friend's floor in the village of Stepaside, worrying for Carrie and his children. Now, as snow fell on his shoulders while he rowed, the cove was chock-a-block with debris, mostly wood from dories, schooners, and buildings. William was afraid he would see a body.

When he hauled his boat up, he met Ben Hollett, who called, "yes, they're safe," before William could even ask. William's tears flowed in rivers and he let out a great sob that filled the harbour. He glanced up at the village and saw Pearl come round the corner of a neighbour's house. "My chair is gone, Daddy!" she cried. "The one you made for me." He ran toward her and pulled her off the ground into his big fisherman's arm. He held her tight as he faced the harbour and surveyed the damage the *tsunami* had caused.

William could see right away that his house was gone. So were his flake and his stage. The Brushetts lost the three barrels of potatoes and two barrels of turnips that would have seen them through the winter. Their five hens were drowned. They'd also lost the four gallons of molasses they'd bought. Gone also was their two tons of coal and two cords of firewood, their means of staying warm from now until spring would break months later. The long wild ride to Bartlett's Island had cost William and Carrie Brushett possessions worth $1,493—everything they owned. All they had left was the forty dollars in William's pocket. But Fred, Lottie, Lillian, Pearl, and James were alive and they only had cuts and bruises.

5

The village of Lawn rises out of a lush valley on the southern end of the Burin Peninsula. According to the local families, the first Europeans to over-winter there were Irish and they enjoyed one of the best fishing harbours on the South Coast. The people fished cod, caplin, salmon, herring, and lobster, which they processed in a factory that employed eight people in 1891. They also ran a seal fishery.

As six-year-old Anna Tarrant lay frozen with fear on the kitchen day bed in her Lawn home, her mother came rushing in from the root cellar, the family tabby behind her. Hilda Murphy Tarrant, a native of St. John's who had married a local man, dropped her carrots and blue potatoes with a great thud. Beneath her the ground shook.

"Mommy!" Anna cried, in spite of her sore throat. Anna's little sister, Elizabeth, and brother, Charles, only two, toddled in. Baby Joe was upstairs in the crib his father had made long ago for the Tarrants' first child. Elizabeth and Charles were too young to be scared of the rumbling itself but they caught sight of the whitening of their mother's face.

"Where's Isadore?" Hilda asked of her oldest child.

Anna shrugged. "I don't know," she whispered. She had been sick all day, drifting in and out of sleep, and hadn't paid too much attention to the comings and goings of her sister and brothers.

Hilda put her hand to her mouth.

"Where's your father?" she cried, looking around the kitchen, seemingly oblivious to the shaking stacks of dishes.

As soon as the rumbling stopped, Pat Tarrant appeared. At forty-three, he was ten years older than his wife. He had been in the Royal Navy as a young man and had witnessed an earthquake in the crystal waters of the Indian Ocean.

"Hilda, get the children in warm clothes and get them to high ground," he ordered. "There's a tidal wave on the way."

"I'm sick, Daddy," Anna said feebly.

"I know, child," her father answered, bending down so that he was face to face with her. "But you have to be brave now. You have to get dressed and put on your winter coat. Then you have to go up the hill with Mommy because there's going to be a big wave come in."

"Pat, what do you mean?" Hilda said. "Will it come all the way in to the houses?"

"It might, maid," her husband answered. "We have to be prepared. I've seen it happen when I was overseas."

Hilda shuddered. Anna hiccupped in fear.

"We have to find Isadore," Hilda said, shoving a fingernail between her teeth.

"Don't worry," Pat said. "I'll get him. I'm going to alert the neighbours anyway. You bundle up the children and take them to the top of the hill as quickly as you can."

In a flash he was gone. Then, as Anna was getting out of her pajamas and into a dress Hilda had fetched from upstairs, her father rushed back into the house. Holding his hand was ten-year-old Isadore, ashen-faced.

"Mommy!" he said, running to Hilda and wrapping his arms around her.

"He was just next door at Victoria and Nick's," Pat said. "He was too afraid to move with the tremors." He turned to his eldest. "You're safe now. Just do what your mother says and help her with the other children." Then he was gone again.

Pat Tarrant went from one house to another on the low land that ringed the harbour, banging on doors and shouting, "There's a tidal wave coming! Get to high ground!" Men and women came out of their houses and watched him knock on their neighbours' doors

"Do you think so, Pat?" they called.

"I do!" he replied, still walking. "I do, I saw it in the Indian Ocean."

He was a respected man and they believed him. They raced back into their houses and pulled babies out of cribs, toddlers out of beds, and wrapped their children in their winter coats. They slammed their doors shut and fixed their eyes on the high land as they made for it as quickly as they could, ignoring the stillness of the water below. There was no wind in the air but Pat Tarrant's words held sway.

With everyone except Kate and Tom Tarrant, an old couple who refused to leave their home which abutted the beach. Distant relatives of Pat's, they did not believe their house was in any danger.

"It's a clear night," sixty-seven-year-old Tom told Anna's father. "I think everything's all right."

"That rumbling is all over now," his sixty-three-year-old wife echoed him. "Everything's fine now."

Pat shook his head; he was certain the old couple was in danger. But there were others to warn, more doors to bang on. He moved on. He looked up from the beach and saw dozens of people streaming out of their houses to the higher ground. Some of them went into dwellings built on the hills around Lawn; others went beyond the houses to even higher land.

As Hilda Tarrant led her children out the door, with her youngest in her arms, she looked behind at a sponge cake on the kitchen counter. She had baked it for Pat's birthday, which was today.

At seven-thirty the water drained out of Lawn harbour, revealing a mass of seaweed over endless grey and blue beach rocks. By now Pat had rejoined his wife and children who were climbing up the hill to the Tarrants' barn.

"Don't look back," Pat told them.

But Anna did and she saw her neighbours' homes go out to sea when a hundred foot wave came in and took them. Then the water withdrew again, leaving two-masted schooners high and dry in the harbour. Around them were splinters of wood from dories, flakes and stages. Pat realized that old Tom and Kate

Tarrant had remained in their home. Even in the dimness of the evening light he could see that their house remained intact. Pat pulled away from Hilda and the children and confided his worry to the men he fished with. With a squeeze of Hilda's shoulder, he hurried down the hill with his dory mates.

"Will you be all right?" she asked.

"I will!" he called. "I think that's the last of it! I'll be back—stay there with the little ones!"

Anna shivered as the darkness drew in. Her throat ached; how she wished for some molasses.

Down below, Pat and the other fishermen waded through icy sea water and debris to reach Tom and Kate Tarrant. Oddly, the fence surrounding the old couple's garden remained standing and the men had to climb over it in their soaking wet clothes. When they opened the Tarrants' door, Kate said, "Thank God!" Then the cries she had been holding in came out full force. Pat picked her up and laid her over his shoulders. The other men carried Tom. The hardest part was getting them over the fence, which they tried to kick down but could not since the water was so heavy. Once they were clear of the sea water, the Tarrants walked up the hill to join the neighbours in the barn. But before he returned, Pat dashed into his own house and retrieved his birthday cake.

There was no loss of life in Lawn, due largely to the efforts of Pat Tarrant. But the property damage was considerable, especially for those families who lived near the beach. Pat Tarrant's own fishing enterprise suffered considerably. His stage was swept away, and his wharf and flake were badly damaged. He lost his trap moorings, five trap kegs, a leader for his trap, a buoy rope, a herring net, and thirty hogsheads of salt. In addition, two tons of coal meant to keep his brood warm over the winter were swept away. As he stood on the shore in the morning, on the spot where his stage had been, he was dumbstuck at his losses. He had been fishing since he was a boy and now, thirty years later, with a wife and five children, it was as if he was starting all over.

The house of Pat's neighbours, Celestine and Jane Edwards, was so badly damaged it would have to be entirely rebuilt. The parents of five young children, the Edwards' food stores were completely gone as well. Jane lamented the loss of the organ she loved to play every evening; getting another one would have to wait—her prized possession had cost $135—and would be hard to come by in any case.

Frederick and Margaret Edwards' house was also beyond repair. The first wave had ripped it from its foundation. Assessing the damage in the dark after the sea had returned to its normal state that night, Fred saw that all the house's concrete pillars were broken. So was the chimney, which lay flat on the soaking ground, ripped right off the rest of the dwelling.

"I expect we'll need twenty or more barrels of cement to rebuild," Fred told Pat Tarrant in the blackness of the night. "Maybe more."

"Yes," Pat nodded. "And a thousand feet of lumber."

Fred shook his head.

"Don't worry," Pat said. "We'll pull together. You'll come through it somehow."

Fred's heart was like lead. His wharf was also beaten up, as was his store. The giant wave had stolen a hogshead of salt, a barrel of flour, and a ton of coal—in the cold month of November. It had also destroyed his stable.

"I don't know," he told Pat.

Young Augustine Murphy was also in need of comfort. At eighteen, he was the sole breadwinner for his thirty-nine-year-old widowed mother, Angela, his fifteen-year-old brother John, and his three little step-siblings. He cracked his knuckles as he paced back and forth on the spot where his flake had been. He hadn't had a particularly successful fishing season and he really couldn't afford a loss of any kind. In fact, his family had virtually no provisions. His stage was rendered useless by the first wave; his moorings destroyed. He'd have to get all that sorted out over the winter for the next fishing season.

The second wave had hauled away their half ton of coal and ten planks Augustine had collected to build a little bridge to his stage and flake, which were now gone anyway. He wiped his forehead when he thought of it. After he surveyed the damage the waves had wrought, he headed home to tell Angela and the children what they faced the winter. He lugged in their barrel of flour but about half of it had been ruined by sea water. Stoney-faced at the news of their losses, Angela turned to the flour and picked through it, trying to salvage what she could.

6

In Lamaline, Herbert Hillier had almost convinced his wife, Nan, that the tremor they had felt on the way from their home in Point au Gaul was nothing to be concerned about. Nan tried to enjoy the Orange Lodge supper in Lamaline with her neighbours from home and their friends in other communities on the bottom of the Burin Peninsula. But, in spite of Herbert's attempts to reassure her, memories of the earth's rumbling nagged at Nan. It didn't help matters that the diners at the Orange Hall talked of nothing else.

At the supper Nan sat next to her sister and brother-in-law from Point au Gaul, Jessie and David Hipditch. Jessie told Nan of the strange vision of her baby, Elizabeth, she had experienced just after the tremor. But with her husband's encouragement she had brushed it off. The Hipditch children, including five-year-old George and three-year-old Henry, were safe with their grandmother, Lizzie Hillier, who was Jessie's mother.

As people arrived at the hall, they brought the fanciful news that the harbour waters had receded way below the normal low tide mark. In fact, the mark kept falling farther back, as if some giant force was sucking the water out of the harbour, so much so that the bottom of the harbour was now exposed for the first time ever. Jessie, David, and Nan rushed outside to see this remarkable phenomenon. The hall was on the highest point of land in Lamaline and they peered down on the dry harbour bottom, amazed to see the smooth stones, dark sand, and reams of seaweed that lay there.

"I never thought I'd see that," David said. A small group that had gathered behind him murmured in agreement. But worry lines crossed their faces as well. Their fears were realized when the water that had disappeared so quietly came barrelling in with the force of a canon ball.

"It's coming in!" Nan heard someone shriek. "It's coming in!"

She clung to Herbert as dusk drew in and they strained to watch the water rise to twenty feet from almost nothing a few moments before. Then a wall of seawater, icy and swift, raced to the houses that clung to the shore. Nan gasped as she saw men and women run away with screaming children in their arms. The ocean flooded the homes they had vacated just in time and swamped the school which had also been built on lower ground. The roads were buried in water as well.

Nan swallowed her breath as she watched the water rise up the hill toward the Orange Hall where she stood as stiff as a marsh bittern. What would they do if the water came up there? But then it stopped, still two hundred yards away, and began to recede. It carried out chicken houses, dories, and fences. The fence posts reminded Nan of matchsticks as they were swept away. The squawking of the poor drowning birds stuck in her ears. She turned to her husband.

"Oh Herbert, what will we do? What about the children?"

His answer was gruff. "Never mind, never mind now," he said. "They'll be all right. Don't be frightened."

But Nan's heart crept up in her chest into her throat and mouth. All around her, women cried and the faces of men grew white as snow. They were deathly afraid for their children in Point au Gaul, High Beach, Taylor's Bay, and Lord's Cove. It would be at least an hour before any of them could get home. They walked in and out of the hall, letting their gravy solidify and their potatoes harden, as they waited for the next onslaught from the Atlantic.

It came, as they knew it would from the behaviour of the sea, but it was not as fierce as the first wave and the houses on the lower ground in Lamaline were empty now. When it receded this time, the people in the Orange Lodge were more confident it would not return and they were right.

Jessie Hipditch had watched the whole thing and could not contain the thumping in her chest. By now, she was convinced the sight of baby Elizabeth on the walk to Lamaline from Point au Gaul was a dark omen, maybe even a token. She pulled on her raven hair as she rushed up to Nan.

"Are you going home?" she asked. "We're going now."

Nan nodded and Herbert agreed. "Don't worry," Herbert told Jessie. "There was enough warning that everyone got out of their houses on time. There's only been property damage."

Jessie's husband, David, joined the trio by now and he gave a quick nod in agreement but Nan could see the worry flush on his face.

"Let's get going," she said.

Out of habit, Herbert picked up their suitcase, which contained only one cake by now. The four of them discussed the safest route home and decided they would stick to high land. They said quick good-byes and left the hall. They crossed the bog on high ground, rather than risk walking through Lamaline itself, on the off-chance that the seawater wasn't done rushing in.

Traversing the bog was hard work and cold in November. All four were soaked to their knees by the time they made it to the road that would take them to Point au Gaul by an inland route. Nan tried to chat, but while Herbert made small talk, she noticed that Jessie and David were silent the whole time. They reached the road first and then walked as fast as they could in bogwater-soaked clothing to their village.

On the way, they passed a Lamaline man with his granddaughter in his arms and his daughter walking wordlessly alongside him. Nan's mind was cloudy and she did not speak to him; five minutes later, she couldn't say if he was an apparition or not.

When Nan and Herbert reached Salmonier Bridge, they stopped. Its great wooden piers had been washed away by the *tsunami*. Farther, what remained of the bridge was tipped at such an angle that they could cross it only by clinging to the rail, which was now on the top of the bridge. The moon bathed the land in a brilliant glow by now and Nan could see Jessie and David on the wrecked structure, quickly pushing on.

"Well, we'll have to cross it, too," Herbert said. Nan nodded. By the time they crossed the creaky bridge, Jessie and David were out of sight. As the harbour came within view, they could see it was chock-a-block with wreckage. It was as if a half dozen ships had gone aground.

"Well, my boat is gone," Herbert said. He sounded nonchalant; indeed, he had expected this after the events he had witnessed in Lamaline, but Nan felt a catch in her throat.

Than a man appeared out of the darkness and shouted, "Stop!"

Nan hesitated; she wanted to ask him what he wanted, but Herbert said, "Never mind, come on!" He had just felt the weight of a boulder in his belly and he suddenly knew that something much worse than property damage had happened in Point au Gaul.

Then he and Nan passed a woman who was moving slowly and crying.

"Did you notice that woman, Herbert?" Nan said. "I wonder why she's crying?"

But Herbert, weighed down by the weight in his stomach, didn't answer. He rushed into the village with his wife. In the moonlight their eyes took in the destruction along the waterfront: the wrecked stages, stores, gears, traps, and boats. Herbert could form no words. Not even the sight of the wave action in Lamaline had prepared him for this. He grabbed Nan's elbow and turned up toward their home.

Nan's brother, Chesley, met them at the gate. Nan saw that he was alone.

"Where are the children?" she screamed.

"They're safe. They're with mother on the hill," he answered quickly. "I brought them up and came back here to meet you."

Nan's body went soft. She hardly heard Chesley explain how he barely had time to get the children to their grandmother's house on high land. Her heart ached for them. She had to see them. She turned to Herbert. "Let's go to the children," she said.

"You can't go, Nan," Chesley said. "The bridge across the brook is gone."

Herbert saw the wetness in his wife's eyes. "You stay here with Chesley and I'll go get the children," he said.

Nan let out a heavy sigh. She went inside to put the kettle on. Even though Chesley told her there had been no damage to the house, she wanted to check for herself. She wondered if Jessie and David's children were all right.

An hour earlier, eight-year-old Ruby Hillier, Nan and Herbert's daughter, had been doing her homework at the kitchen table. Her brothers Leslie and Lawson sat alongside her: ten-year-old Leslie doing his sums and five-year-old Lawson doodling on a slate. Their uncle Chesley had already put the baby to bed.

All of a sudden Ruby heard a thunderous noise, not unlike the one that had accompanied the earth tremor earlier that evening. Ruby jumped up from her chair and ran to the window where she raised the blind and peered into the dusk. She blinked at the sight that greeted her; it was a white mass tumbling toward her house.

"Oh my!" Ruby cried. "Look at the sheep!"

She was stunned at how fast they were moving. They were half way up the meadow across the road from their house.

Chesley joined his niece at the window.

"I don't believe they're sheep," he said as it dawned on him that his niece had mistaken the foamy whitecaps of the huge waves for sheep. Moments later sea water surrounded the Hillier home.

Then the general panic began. From outside, Ruby heard a roar. Chesley ran into the back bedroom to fetch baby Cyril. With the child in his left arm, Chesley shooed Ruby and the boys out the door. The little group stopped dead at the front door; the porch was filled with frigid water. They stepped gingerly over it and managed to keep their feet dry. Then they rushed up the hill, Uncle Chesley looking behind constantly. He feared another wall of water was on its way.

Near the top of the hill, they met their grandfather, whose face was wet with tears.

"Grandpa, what's wrong?" Ruby asked. "What's the matter?"

The old man didn't answer, but Chesley said, "I don't know. I suppose he's confused."

When the group reached the safety of the high ground, Ruby looked at the village below. It was empty of people, all of whom had rushed to the top of the hill. But the little girl's face whitened at what she saw. The harbour was blocked with broken boats, stages and flakes that had crashed into the water, and houses that the giant wave had torn down. On top of the hill old Mrs. Collins stood making the sign of the cross. Her family was gathered around her, intoning the "Hail Marys" of the rosary. Three-year-old Magdalen Collins sat at her grandmother's feet; the child was wet to her hips with sea water.

"I'll never forget this sight," Ruby told her older brother, Leslie. "I wonder if anyone died."

Leslie said nothing but bit his bottom lip in response.

7

As Herbert Hillier made his way up the hill to make sure his four children were safe he made one gasp after another at the destruction that greeted him. Where his father-in-law Henry's house had stood, there was now a barren space. Herbert stopped in his tracks and looked around; Henry's stage was gone, too, and so was his store. Even the old man's fence had disappeared. Herbert was gobsmacked. Henry had lived in that house as long as anyone could remember, for most, if not all, of his sixty-eight years and now there was no evidence that it had even existed.

The hairs on Herbert's head rose and his body shook. Then his legs began moving again. He had to get up the hill to make sure the children were all right. But then he was struck with a horrific thought: where was Henry? Had he gone to the Temperance meeting that had been planned for this evening? He usually did, he was an active member. And where was Lizzie, Henry's wife? She was Jessie's mother, too, and Jessie had left the children with her for the night. Herbert shuddered now as he thought of Jessie and her husband, David Hipditch, racing through the darkness from the Orange Lodge meeting in Lamaline to Point au Gaul.

He plodded on with fear in every step. When he reached his mother's house he threw the door open to hear wailing. He ran inside and flashed his eyes around to take in each of his children. He let out a whoosh of air when he saw them all, safe and warm. But the tears...

"Nan and Jessie's mother is dead," said his own mother. "Washed away."

"Grandma is gone!" Ruby cried.

"But that's not the worst of it," old Mrs. Hillier wailed. "Jessie's three children are gone."

Herbert couldn't move.

"What? The three of them?" he said. "Gone?"

"The three of them, swept away," his mother answered. "Thomas, Henry, and Elizabeth, the baby that she was still nursing."

Ruby emitted a great sob.

"What are we going to do, Daddy?" she cried.

Her father's tongue was thick.

"Well," he said finally, "we're going to go home to your mother and help her and Aunt Jessie out."

He went to the porch to fetch his children's winter clothes. Then he turned back to his mother.

"Is Henry all right?" he asked. "Did Henry get swept away too?"

"Well, that's the only bit of good news," came the reply. "He was at the Temperance meeting so he's alive."

Herbert nodded, though his heart was no lighter.

"Herbert," his mother said. "There's more, though."

Herbert tilted his head in her direction. What else could there possibly be after the disaster of all disasters that had befallen Jessie and David?

"Young Irene is dead, too," his mother said. "She was down visiting her grandmother, as you know, and she got swept away with her little cousins."

"Good God," said Herbert as he envisioned another of Nan's nieces, the daughter of her other sister, Jemima. "How old was she again?"

"She was eleven," his mother answered. "Jemima will go mad. Irene was her only daughter with all those boys. Point au Gaul will never be the same after this, Herbert."

"No," Herbert said as his children put on their boots. "No."

Ruby sniffled as she thought of Irene drowning. Irene used to sit behind her in school. The girl was her favourite cousin.

"We'd best get home," her father said, placing his hand on her shoulder.

"Good night, children," their only living grandmother called. "God bless you."

Nan's grip on her tea cup was tight while she waited for the children. Chesley paced the living room. He knew something of the deaths and destruction that had visited Point au Gaul that night but he didn't want to be the one to tell Nan; he thought that duty should fall to her husband. He thought also that the family should be together when she was informed of the many likely deaths among her kin. Silence hung heavy as they waited.

Suddenly the door burst open and Nan's brother, Tom, ran in, his face covered in red patches.

Nan ran out to the porch to meet him.

"What's wrong, Tom?" she asked, her heart thumping loudly again.

He pulled her to him and sobbed.

"Don't you know Mother is gone?" he cried. "Father's home is gone, too!"

Nan drew in air and let it out in a great cry.

"Oh no!" she sobbed. "Oh no!" The tears poured down her face as she and Tom hugged each other like survivors on a raft.

Then Tom told her that their sister Jessie's children had all been swept away.

Nan howled at the news and fell into a chair. Jemima's daughter, Irene, was gone as well, he said. She rocked back and forth, her arms folded across her chest.

Then Jessie and David opened the door and came in. Jessie's clothes were drenched, even her long dark hair was dripping cold water.

"I want my baby," she said. "My children are gone. I want to know what happened to Thomas and Henry. I'm nursing Elizabeth..."

David stood like a fencepost, his eyes sunken and blank.

"She keeps talking like that," he said. "And I can't keep her indoors."

Nan took Jessie in her arms and for ten long minutes both sisters cried from deep in their bellies. Afterwards it seemed that Jessie's babbling had ceased. But then she said that she had to nurse Elizabeth. Nan took her upstairs and began to undress her and dry her off.

Downstairs, the men stood in the living room, saying nothing. Before long they heard Jessie scream about her lost children. She demanded to know what had happened to them and why they weren't safe. When there were silences they knew Nan was talking softly to her. Then Jessie shouted again, wanting to know every detail of how they had been torn from their grandmother's home and why. David put his hand to his mouth and closed his eyes.

"Sit down, David," Tom said gently.

Upstairs, Nan begged Jessie to quieten down.

By now, Herbert had returned home with his and Nan's four children. They sat on the day bed in the kitchen, like ducks in a row, too afraid to move or say anything. Herbert sent Tom to fetch Nan's father, Henry, so that the old man could be with his daughters and son in his grief.

Soon Henry was sitting in Nan's kitchen with his grandchildren, listening to Jessie's mournful cries. After awhile, Ruby went upstairs and sat outside Nan's room where her Aunt Jessie lay. She crouched down and prayed for her dead cousins but mostly for Aunt Jessie. Now Ruby knew what they meant by the phrase "hell on earth."

Herbert and Tom settled David in the Hillier kitchen with cups of tea and lassie bread. As he spread the molasses on the bread, Herbert felt guilty that his wife's kitchen was untouched, that his floors were dry. But there was little time for emotional indulgences. He and Tom quickly went to the porch and put their rubber boots on. They had decided to go out and see what could be done. By now, Herbert deeply regretted going to the Orange Lodge supper in Lamaline when he might have been of some assistance to his own village. There was no way of predicting what would befall Point au Gaul, he knew, but perhaps he shouldn't have dismissed the earth tremor as he did. It was obvious now that it had something to do with the great waves that had swept houses, fishing rooms, and women and children away.

As he and Tom picked their way through the wreckage that was strewn through Point au Gaul, Tom told him what had happened in his absence. The first wave had rolled in on the flat land of the village and lifted houses and stores off their foundations, smashing them to bits. It swept the entire waterfront clean, carrying virtually everything there out to sea. It was the first wave that had taken Henry and Lizzie Hillier's house out to sea and with it, Lizzie, and her four grandchildren.

On the opposite end of the beach on a neck of land, the first wave—the one that young Ruby Hillier mistook for sheep—splintered an old two-storey house. Two women, eighty-five-year-old Mary Ann Walsh and sixty-year-old Elizabeth Walsh lived there together. One of the women was killed in the initial crash while the other was pulled out to sea.

"They say Thomas Hillier is missing, too," Tom said of his neighbour with the same name, the fish oil inspector.

Herbert shook his head.

"He wasn't even supposed to be home," Tom continued. "He wanted to come home for his birthday and have a party. It was the first time in his life he ever wanted one, well, since he was a child anyway. Young Caroline was running around earlier talking of how they were making two cakes. She was so excited about it. Now they're out looking for him. He went out to haul his boat up before the first wave came."

"How's Lydia?" Herbert asked of Thomas' wife.

"Well," Tom answered, his brow knitted, "she has another baby due soon."

Herbert shook his head again.

"I'm very sorry for your mother," he said suddenly.

Tom nodded.

By now they had reached a group of men who were looking for bodies. It was a difficult task given the amount of debris clogging the beach and harbour. They broke into small groups and assigned each other sections of ground to cover. They were confident by now that the erratic tidal action was over and the bright moonlight was helpful to them as they went about their grim task.

Two of the men found Thomas Hillier's body at ten o'clock. Water-logged and leaden, it took four of them to carry the body to the hall.

"Right where his boat would have been," said Herbert. "It's the strangest thing. Was he dragged out and brought back in? Or hit on the head by a piece of wood?"

"There wasn't a mark on him," Tom answered. "He obviously stayed out too long. He tried too hard to get his boat to safety."

"He wasn't a fisherman," Herbert muttered. "He wasn't around the water as much as the rest of us. Perhaps he wasn't as afraid of it as we are..."

At the hall, pregnant Lydia cried over the body of her husband. She pushed her large tummy to the side and lay her chest and head on him as he reclined lifeless on the table. She could not hear the sobs that rippled through the hall for her and her fatherless unborn child. At her side, her daughter, Caroline, sniffled for the birthday party that would never happen. She kept thinking of an incident from earlier that night. Before supper, her high-spirited father had thrown a stone into a pool of water and splashed mud on his jacket. At home, as the family's potatoes boiled on the stove top, Caroline had asked him, "Father, may I brush the mud off your jacket?" Thomas had turned to his daughter and answered quietly, "Yes dear, you do that as you may never get the chance again."

Not long afterwards the men came across the body of Nan's sixty-six-year-old mother, Lizzie. She was not far along the beach from Thomas Hillier, making the villagers think that she might have died from injuries sustained in the initial crash of the first wave, although there were none visible to the naked eye. Very soon afterwards, Herbert and the other men found the little bodies of Jessie's three children, Thomas, Henry, and baby Elizabeth. Three-year-old Henry, clad in his pajamas, was lying in the house of a motorized dory trapped in the landwash. His hands were curled around the rails as if he were trying to save himself; it was obvious he had survived the impact of the first wave and was trying his best to live. The men who found him buried their faces in their hands and tried to stifle the sounds of their grief.

After finding the children and bringing them to the hall, the men gave up searching for the night. They knew young Irene Hillier was still out there, and so were the Walsh women, but they were too tired and grief-stricken to continue. They simply could not take anymore.

8

As the awful day of November 18, 1929 ended, the people of Point au Gaul counted their dead. They began to wonder, too, how many had died in the neighbouring villages and towns along the coast. Many of them had friends and relatives in nearby Lamaline, where Nan and Herbert Hillier and Jessie and David Hipditch had journeyed for their aborted supper at the Loyal Orange Lodge. Mayhem had broken out when Lamaline harbour had emptied of water. Further panic had ensued when the harbour and the lower parts of the village itself had bulged with sea water, the result of a great crush of a wave and then another wave.

Lamaline first appeared in French maps in 1620 as *Cap de la Meline*. The French name *La Maligne*, directly translated as "evil" or "wicked," likely refers to the difficulty of landing a boat in the harbour there because of the many shoals and the low-lying, flat, almost swampy land. In 1763 Captain Cook charted the South

Coast of Newfoundland, looking for suitable sites for fishing settlements; one of those chosen was Lamaline.

Despite the early French connection, the first European settlers
came from England and Ireland. Lamaline had a significant population
by the early 1800s; in 1807, Reverend John Harries of the Society for
the Propagation of the Gospel baptized seventy-five souls, one-third of
whom were adults and "many very old." Harries was the first clergy-
man in Lamaline and the only one most of the livyers had ever seen.

Conflict with the French was ongoing. In 1827 the residents of
Lamaline appealed to Newfoundland Governor Thomas Cochrane
for help, claiming "the French constantly fish on our shore on
Sundays (presumably the Newfoundlanders' day of rest) with
boats from sixty to a hundred in number—have taken our dry fish
from the beach—have lately burned a boat belonging to one of us
and stolen his wharf posts..." Their petition was successful in win-
ning the sympathy of the governor. He immediately dispatched the
British naval vessel HMS *Manly* to patrol the coast. The people of
Lamaline sent Cochrane a gift of fish in thanks.

While they portrayed the French as their enemies in this
instance, in reality the ties between the two groups were far more
complicated than that. Lamaline fishermen sold caplin to the
French in contravention of the law. Some tension arose when
Captain Alexander Milne of HMS *Crocodile* discovered the illegal
sales as well as considerable smuggling of liquor from St. Pierre to
Newfoundland. The French tried to convince him with a taste test
that the Newfoundland caplin tasted much better than their
own—they failed. All hands breathed sighs of relief when Milne
decided not to arrest anyone, but to issue warnings instead.

*

The Loyal Orange Lodge, perched on a hill overlooking Lamaline, was at the centre of social life. Catholics of the town were welcome there, too—in small communities dominated by a harsh North Atlantic environment sectarianism was a luxury they could not indulge. As Jessie, David, Nan, and Herbert fled the hall, they left behind people as dumbfounded and fear-filled as they were. Most of the Lamaline people who had been in the hall left their dinners uneaten and rushed to their homes, heading straight to their children's bedrooms. They plucked their children from sleep and scurried to higher ground with them.

Twenty-six-year-old Melinda Hillier held her three children close to her as her husband, Frederick, kept a watch on the ocean, waiting for the next wave. Melinda herself could not bear to look. Her ribs rocked as her heart pounded in her chest. Wilomena Emberley, the same age as Melinda, escaped with her brood of five. Like quite a few Lamaline men, Wilomena's husband, Henry, was in Corner Brook, working on the giant mill and townsite under construction there. It was a great chance to put a few dollars in his pocket. But now, alone with the children, Wilomena ached for him as she watched the first wave batter their house. She knew from the whipping sound the wave made as it hit the dwelling that they wouldn't sleep there that night and that repairing it would be a real job. As she pushed down her own sob, her youngest started to cry and Wilomena pulled the child to her breast. "Shhh," she said. "It'll be all over soon. You're safe." Then she bit her own lip so hard it bled.

Jane Hillier's husband was also at Corner Brook. She had two boys, Fred and Cyril, who fished with their father now, and four younger children. Jane had been terror-struck to see the harbour run dry from her station outside the Hall with her friends and neighbours, who also stood mesmerized. Down below, her oldest sons rushed their younger siblings out of the house, realizing that it was dangerously near the beach and acting on instinct. As their toddler brother, Stanley, ambled out, Fred picked him up under his arm, despite the child's protests, and pushed each of the other children from behind, trying to hurry them to higher ground. By now, Jane was running toward them.

"Go back up the hill, Mother!" Cyril called. "We're coming!"

When they reached the top of the hill where Jane stood waiting, glassy-eyed, for her children, the first wave drove in and smashed their house to pieces. Jane let out a wail. When the wave hauled back, Fred saw the fence fall down, the family's fishing store flow out with the sea, and their trawls and rope unfurl in the water. The cash their father was earning would come in handy, he thought. They would lose just about everything, he knew, including his quintal of Madeira fish. Jane was thinking of the twenty pounds of pork she had stored away and the coal that was meant to keep them warm the winter.

Not far away, on the grasses of the hill, young bride Gertrude Caines felt her face grow hot with tears. She was twenty-one and not long married to Leslie Caines, a thirty-year-old fisherman, who had grievously injured his hand. Leslie was no longer able to fish and Gertrude was wasting away with worry. They had five dollars a week from Public Charities but it was not enough and moreover, it was not what Leslie wanted and certainly not what she wanted. Gertrude spent the entire summer bent over the dark earth, coaxing potatoes, carrots, turnips, beets, and cabbage out of the soil. As the July fog hung, she spread caplin on her garden, having gathered the little fish from the beaches herself. As September approached, she went among her burgeoning crops in the dusk and prayed to the Blessed Virgin Mary. Now, on the night of November 18, 1929, Gertrude knew, all her vegetables were gone.

9

Two waves had reached into Point au Gaul on the bottom of the Burin Peninsula, swamping the village and taking the lives of Jessie and David's three young children, Jessie's mother, Lizzie, the two Walsh women, Thomas Hillier, and young Irene Hillier.

The men of Point au Gaul had recovered most of the bodies under brilliant moonlight the night of the *tsunami* but some were still missing the next day, including Irene Hillier and Mary Ann Walsh. That same strange night, a horse that had been swept out to sea swam back and walked onto dry land with no ill effects.

On November 19, 1929, the day after the tidal wave, a southeast wind came up. It churned the sea higher and higher, whipping up another panic in the village. The whitecaps brought wreckage back to the beach and right up to the remaining houses. The wind and waves also carried Mary Ann's body to a small island on the other side of the neck of land on which her house had been situated.

The men and boys scoured the beaches of Point au Gaul but they could not find Irene's body. Every family prayed that it would be delivered. Irene's mother, Jemima, could not sleep; night after night she sat up at her bedroom window, listening to the waves and the wind. "It's awfully cold for Irene out there," she said repeatedly of her only daughter. Her husband, Joshua, who went to look for Irene at dawn every morning, tried to cajole his wife into bed but she would not rest. "I can't sleep till she's found," Jemima said between her tears.

The bodies were all laid out in the hall, ironically built on high ground. Nan Hillier did not go to see her mother's body. She did not see Jessie's children either. "You'll want to remember them as they are," Herbert told her. "It'll be too upsetting to see them any other way." Besides, Nan was too busy tending to Jessie who still babbled and veered into hysteria.

Now homeless, David and Jessie moved in with Nan and Herbert. David's dory was swept away, as was his stage and fishing gear. He would have to start his fishing enterprise from scratch. The Hipditches had lost most of their winter provisions as well, but that meant nothing, compared to the loss of their children.

The village held a joint funeral for Lizzie and her four grandchildren, including the missing Irene. But Jemima could find no comfort in the ritual, nor in the constant expressions of sympathy that came from her neighbours in Point au Gaul—not as long as Irene was out there somewhere.

The day after the funeral Lizzie's spinning wheel, which she had been using the day of the *tsunami*, washed up on the Point au Gaul beach. It was intact and Nan took it into her own home to keep/A day later, a child playing in a small brook about a hundred yards inland found a prize teapot that Lizzie once owned. The teapot lid was missing but there wasn't a chip out of the pot.

The newly widowed Lydia Hillier, too, grieved heavily, even as she awaited the birth of her third child. She also faced a practical problem in that the main source of her family income was gone. Her nineteen-year-old stepson, Harold, would have to be the breadwinner now. But Harold's store and fishing gear had been swept away. And she worried that relations with her stepchildren were not always smooth. This was their house first, Lydia reminded herself worriedly, before she married their father. She reached far inside herself to comfort Caroline who cried ceaselessly for her father. Little Ben was so quiet it worried Lydia. Still a toddler, he was too young for her to know how much he understood. At least I still have my children, Lydia kept telling herself.

Her neighbour, John Walsh, no longer had anything. The sixty-six-year-old bachelor was in poor health but had somehow managed to jog up the hill to safety before the first wave cracked his little dwelling in two. Then it turned the clapboard into splinters and carried it out to sea. John Walsh turned around from the top of the hill with tears streaming down his ruddy fisherman's cheeks. He had no bed now, he knew, no bedclothes, no sugar or tea, no stove to cook on or keep him warm. He had only the clothes on his back. He saw that, in addition to his house, his stage was demolished. He knew that his trawl lines would be gone, too, as would his 140-fathom, nine-inch manila rope. Where was his boat? He figured that was wrecked too. At his age, he'd have to start all over, somehow.

*

Sixty-eight-year-old Manuel and sixty-one-year-old Jessie Inkpen had spent their whole lives in Stepaside, Burin, a little cove named after the home village of its first English settlers. The Inkpens had prospered and lived in a ten room, three-storey house, built near the water. By November of 1929, Manuel was in poor health and increasingly dependent on Jessie and on Bertha, their live-in maid.

Bertha had gone out visiting for the evening and the couple was having a cup of tea after their supper of fish and brewis when the first wave struck Stepaside. Manuel and Jessie found themselves knee-deep in gelid salt water as they sat at their kitchen table, and stood, shocked at the cold on their legs.

"My God!" Jessie cried.

"We'd best get out," said Manuel, still holding his cup of tea.

"Shall we bring anything?" Jessie asked. "Shall we put our coats on?"

"I don't think so, dear," her husband answered. "I think we better get moving quickly before the water rises up."

Their legs already numb with cold, they pushed one foot in front of the other, until they reached the back door, the one nearest the kitchen. Jessie, stronger than her husband at this stage in their lives, pushed against it and heaved. It opened and they stepped onto a flake, their own.

"It seems steady," she said to Manuel. "Come on."

She regretted listening to Manuel and not taking his cane.

As soon as the elderly couple stood on the flake it pushed off from the shore and floated to sea.

"Good God!" said Manuel.

Jessie's face whitened. Her eyes scanned the village. Flakes and stages were destroyed. Dories were bottom up or cut in two as if giant knives had come down from the heavens. Cords of fire-wood drifted alongside the flake that had become their raft. Were they going to die like this? Jessie decided she had to do some-thing.

"Help!" she cried. "Someone help us!"

"Help!" Manuel joined her.

"Don't strain yourself, dear," Jessie said gently. She worried about the effect of this on his health. She never imagined they'd be floating out in the bay on a flake in November.

"Help!" she yelled again.

Men began appearing from the houses on the high ground. Jessie saw them point to the old couple on the flake in the middle of the cove. In spite of her predicament, she almost smiled.

Manuel was looking behind them, out to sea.

"I wonder will there be another flood?" he said.

"Hush, now," Jessie answered. "Our neighbours are on their way to rescue us. See how they're getting a dory out?"

Manuel nodded. He had begun to shiver. Jessie, too, was chilled and could not feel her feet. Then the water began to rise again and the boards of the flake began to creak. The swell broke the flake in two, throwing Manuel and Jessie into the sea. Jessie screamed and trod water madly, trying to find bottom. Manuel was too stunned to speak but his feet, as numb as they were, found the sea floor. He raised a frozen arm to grab hold of Jessie but she was too far away, still screaming. Then she stopped.

"I'm all right!" she called out. "I can stand up! On my toes!"

"My God!" said Manuel. How long could they last like this? The sight of his wife's face pointed at the sky, her hair covered in cold ocean water, tore at him.

"Hold onto a plank," Manuel cried. "It'll keep you afloat."
He saw Jessie clutch one and gasp in relief as she did so.

"Are they still coming?" she called.

"They are," said Manuel. "They're almost here."

Two Stepaside men hauled Jessie first and then Manuel into the dory when it arrived alongside the flake. The men rowed quickly to the beach, casting worried glances at their frozen passengers. Then they carried the Inkpens ashore and up a steep bank to a large house where most of their neighbours fearfully waited for more flooding.

Bertha was already there when Jessie and Manuel were carried in.

"A fine night for a cruise," the maid said, her face wet with tears.

"Terrible flooding," Manuel said, his face grey. "Our kitchen floor is all wet."

"Mr. Inkpen," said Bertha. "Didn't you see the big wave? It was monstrous. Sure, it took all the stages and flakes out!"

As the women took off Jessie's stockings and slippers and dried her feet, one of the men said, "The big wave is after receding again and will be back again soon. All the houses and everything on lower ground is in danger of being swept away."

"Oh my goodness," said Jessie. "I didn't realize it was that bad."

"It's just as well you didn't," said Bertha. "There'd be no point to it, the situation you were in."

The women took blankets off the stove and wrapped Manuel and Jessie in them. They pushed hot toddies into their hands and urged them to drink.

"Here it comes!" someone called from the window. "Here comes the wave!"

The villagers rushed outdoors to watch the wall of water crush the Inkpens' home and virtually every stage and flake in Stepaside. The roar startled Manuel this time and the reality of his experience caused his heart to flutter and pearls of sweat to pour down his face. Still seated, he grabbed Jessie's hand. Besides their house, furniture, linen, crockery, and clothing, the sea took Manuel's wharf, barn, two stores, and fishing gear. The old couple's sheep and ten hens drowned as well.

When Manuel learned all this after the second wave pulled back, he sobbed into Jessie's breast.

"I'm too old for this," he cried.

10

S arah Rennie of Lord's Cove fed her youngest children, Rita, Patrick, Margaret, and Bernard, their supper. They gobbled down their vegetables—hers were good eaters, not like some children in the village, thank God—and happily chewed their salt fish. They knew some lassie bread was waiting if they ate it all, that was her promise.

Sarah kept some potatoes, carrots, and fish in the pot for her husband, Patrick, and her older sons, Martin and Albert. She hadn't expected them home, this being a special night for the Lord's Cove men to get together for cards. Every bit of time away from work was deserved for them; for her, too, when it came, as it occasionally did. Patrick's two missing fingers were testimony to his own diligence. She knew she wouldn't see him till the wee hours. She expected the boys home much earlier than that, though. Albert had school tomorrow, she had reminded him as they headed out with their father.

"Don't be late now," she had said.

Four-year-old Margaret had barely swallowed her lassie bread when her head began to loll.

"Upstairs for you, little maid," Sarah said, gathering the child in her arms. When she came downstairs from tucking her youngest daughter in her cot, Sarah returned to her sewing machine. Baby Bernard was still not tired—he rarely was, Sarah sighed—so she secured him in his high chair and gave him his rattle again. "Bababa," he said as he banged it on the wooden tray.

"You two should get at your lessons now" Sarah said to Rita and young Patrick, running a line of blue thread into the bobber on her Singer.

Just then the sound of thunder drowned out her children's responses and Sarah's skirts were anchored in icy water. She screamed, her eyes wide in horror. Sarah could not scream again because she was suddenly immersed in a mountainous wave. Her house was borne out on the water, heading for the Atlantic. Then the wave returned and threw it into the middle of The Pond with a great heartless thud.

The noise had drawn Patrick Rennie from Prosper Walsh's house and he now stood on a hill above the village with his heart ripped in two. "My wife and children are in there!" he screamed, tearing the lining of his throat.

"They're all drowned," one fisherman whispered to another.

"Yes, they'd have to be," his friend agreed grimly.

The men put their arms around Patrick's strong shoulders, but then he disappeared like a shot, followed by his sons, Martin and Albert. All three ran toward The Pond, stopping abruptly at the shore.

"Sarah!" Patrick called out.

"Mom!" the boys cried. "Mom! Rita!"

"Sarah, answer me! Sarah!"

But there only came silence. Behind them the harbour was empty of sea water, its rocky bottom entirely exposed. The moon was luminous, throwing whiteness throughout the village.

Patrick ran back and forth on the shore of The Pond. Like most fishermen, he could not swim; there had never been any time for such leisure in the summer. He tore at his hair. The meaning of the silence ate into him, devouring his soul.

"Sarah!" he cried.

"Get out of there!" someone called suddenly.

Martin glanced at the dry harbour bottom and realized that another wave might be on its way.

"Come on, Dad," he said firmly, taking his father by the elbow. The boy had no intention of losing his father. Slowly and in a stupor Patrick backed away from The Pond. But as he walked up the hill, he kept looking back at what was now the graveyard of his family.

For the past five years, eighteen-year-old Mary Walsh of Lord's Cove had worked in a hotel in St. Pierre during the winter and spring and helped a French woman there raise her three children. Every summer she returned home to make fish for her father. Mary's mother had died not too long before from an illness that had plagued her for years, leaving Mary and her younger brother, Bertram, motherless. Like most Roman Catholics, Mrs. Walsh had left this life with a lighted candle in her clasped hands, supported by the loving hands of a stronger relative. Mary's mother had expired before the candle had burned more than an inch down. It was a memory that seared Mary's young brain.

That year, 1929, Mary was late going back to St. Pierre, so on a November night she saw the rocky harbour bottom for the first time in her life.

"Pop!" she called out from the front porch. "There's no water in the cove. It's all rocks."

"What?" her father, Jim, answered incredulously.

"Come and see!" Mary insisted.

As soon as her father joined her in the doorway, they saw the first wave coming. All around them, people were running around shouting frantically. The wave seemed as if it was coming from the sky, it was so high. As it came closer, it seemed to pick up speed. Its nasty edge was unmistakable.

Mary's head spun round when her father ran back into the house and upstairs. She fought back panic. Everyone else was running away from their houses to higher ground. Mary stood frozen to the linoleum in the porch, her breathing shallow. What should she do? What was her father doing?

Then Jim rushed back down the stairs, his footfalls heavy on the steps. In his hands was the candle that had led Mary's mother to the afterlife. Mary's eyes glistened with moisture, the roar of the wave outside almost forgotten. Wordlessly, Jim jumped into his boots and went out to the bank where the capstan was and stuck the candle down in a piece of chain. Mary watched him light it and back away. Then he turned and ran, grabbed his daughter, and rushed her to the hills above the village.

As the second wave hit Lord's Cove, the candle remained lit, a tiny fleck of light surrounded by wild waves that somehow did not come close to it. The little light did not go out even as the third wave roared into the beach and demolished flakes, stages, dories, skiffs, and houses.

The *tsunami* did untold damage in Lord's Cove, affecting virtually every family. The men wondered how they would fish next spring. Tusa Chappalla, John Collier, Francis Ferrie, David Fitzpatrick, James Fitzpatrick, Thomas Hodge, and William Lamb were among the many whose stages were ripped to bits by the waves. Other fishermen—Martin Fitzpatrick, Clement Harnett, John Herlidan, Frederick Hennebury, Clotaire Isaacs, and Eugene Papail among them— lost their dories and trap skiffs as well as their stages and stores.

The women saw that from now on even curing fish would be a problem, since some of beaches were washed away. One of these belonged to Prosper Walsh, who had done so much to warn people of the coming disaster. Prosper, with a wife and four dependent children, had built up his eight foot high beach with a wooden and rock breakwater, costing him $150.00. The *tsunami* washed it all away. Even more worrying, the giant waves seemed to have robbed the forty-six-year-old man of his eyesight. As the last wave receded, so did Prosper's vision, so that from then on he saw everything through a blur.

Upstairs in the Rennie house, four-year-old Margaret had been slipping into the heaviness of nighttime sleep when the first wave approached. She lazily turned her head on the pillow her mother, Sarah, had puffed up for her, and glanced at the lamp that burned at the head of the stairs. Then the house shook as if ten gales were bearing down on it and the lamp went out. Margaret felt the shock of a frigid wetness and then nothing.

The three waves that slammed into Lord's Cove were between sixteen and fifty feet high. They hit the harbour at almost 130 kilometres an hour, clearing the little cove of everything it had held.

The Rennie house, containing Margaret, her mother, Sarah, and siblings Rita, Patrick, and Bernard, was dragged into the harbour and then thrown back into The Pond, where it now lay, half-submerged. Patrick Sr., Sarah's husband, howled, half-mad, at the top of the hill, where his friends had led him. His surviving sons, Martin and Albert, stood hollow-faced by his side, too stunned to speak. Every few minutes Albert balled his hands and rubbed his eyes as if he could change the sight in front of him by doing so.

After the third wave the sea returned to its pre-*tsunami* calmness, the very state that had deceived them so. The moon enveloped the still cove in a light that seemed strangely protective, though it revealed the splinters that had been stages and flakes and now clogged up the harbour. When an hour had passed with no sign of another wave, Patrick's friend, John Joe Fitzpatrick, turned to him and said, "I think we'll try and get to your house."

Another neighbour, Herb Fitzpatrick, nodded in agreement. "It's calm now, Pat," he said. "And I expect it'll stay that way."

"We'll do what we can, Pat," John Joe added.

He patted Martin and Albert on the shoulders as he began to move down the hill, Herb by his side.

"Mind your old man, boys," he called back.

Martin and Albert closed in on their father. They were still numb with shock themselves.

As they neared The Pond, the men met Jim Walsh, who had lost virtually nothing to the waves, thanks to his wife's death candle. Jim had just come from Fred Hennebury's property where the two men had tried in vain to recover the bodies of Hennebury's sheep. The animals had been swept away by one of the waves and then pushed under a fishing store on the next incoming wave. They were barred in by a boat that got jammed there by the final wave. All the sheep drowned.

Jim was desperate to help his neighbours, but was at a loss as to how. Herb and John Joe told him they needed a boat to put in The Pond to go out to the Rennie house.

"Mine is all in one piece," Jim said. "We just have to get it hauled over there."

Adrenalin pumped through the men's veins as they lugged the dory across the beach and over the scrap of land to The Pond. Other fishermen carried the oars. Then the three of them, John Joe, Jim, and Herb, jumped into the dory and rowed to the house tilting in the water, their hearts galloping in fear. When they reached it they saw that the cold water came up to the ceiling of the first floor. From the shore of The Pond, they heard a woman scream.

Suddenly, the house rose up as if to make their task easier. Pond and sea water drained out of it, followed by pots, pans, and even table legs. Then they saw the high chair, horizontal and still holding baby Bernard. John Joe reached in the broken window and pulled the chair toward the dory, trying to keep as steady as he could. The sound of his own breathing was all he could hear as he cut the child from the chair and passed him to Herb, who had removed his coat to wrap little Bernard in. They found Rita next, and then her brother, Patrick. Their mother, Sarah, was under the kitchen table, next to the sewing machine—it seemed she did not even have time to move away from her perch.

Only young Margaret was missing. The men could see clearly through the first floor of the house and she was not there. They decided to row back to shore with their sad, sad cargo.

As villagers carried the Rennie family bodies out of Jim Walsh's dory, sobs rang through the harbour. In the hall on top of the hill that marks the western entrance to Lord's Cove, women were already preparing a long table to receive the bodies of Sarah and her children for waking. Their husbands would gather enough planks to make one large and four smaller coffins.

Patrick Rennie had joined the crowd on the shore of The Pond by now. He covered his mouth as he saw the remains of his wife and children lovingly placed in blankets to be taken to the hall.

"Where's Margaret?" he said.

John Joe, Herb, and Jim looked at each other, not knowing what to say.

"We have to have Margaret," Patrick persisted.

Wordlessly, the three men re-entered Jim's dory and rowed back out to the house. The moon seemed even brighter now, if that were possible. They circled the Rennie dwelling, contemplating their next move.

"She might be at the bottom of The Pond, the poor little thing," Herb said.

"I don't think so," said Jim, though he didn't know where this thought came from.

Then John Joe's face lit up.

"I know! She's upstairs!" he cried. "She's upstairs!"

Over the next half hour, they got another dory into The Pond and used pressure to sink the house again so that the floor of the second storey was level with the water. Then they saw the cot where Margaret would surely be found. It was covered in choco-late-coloured mud and seaweed.

"I'll go in and get her little body," Jim said.

"Tread carefully," Herb cautioned. "Or the whole house will go topsy-turvy."

Jim reached into the crib, pushed away the debris the ocean had churned up, and took the little girl's body. As he carried her to the dory, he thought he heard her sigh. He looked at her face and thought she was a bit pink for a child who had drowned. Perhaps... He rushed her to the small boat and the waiting men.

"I think she might be alive!" he said excitedly.

Herb and John Joe crowded in on Margaret. They peeled off their coats and wrapped them around the child as tightly as they could. Jim rocked her and blew hot air on her face as the other two men rowed as fast as they could. Once onshore he ran with her in his arms to John Joe's house.

"I think she's alive!" he cried, hurrying past a row of anxious people in the hallway. "Get some warm water! Quick!"

When Alberta Fitzpatrick eased Margaret into the tub of warm water the child suddenly woke and screamed. At the sound of her voice, everyone in the house, and then Lord's Cove itself, made the joyful noise their hearts had longed to make. Their child had been saved.

11

B en and Beatrice Hollett had watched open-mouthed on the shore of Kelly's Cove as the giant wave reached in and picked up their neighbour's house and carried it out to sea. Inside, Carrie Brushett and her five children felt as if the house were flying and Carrie had somehow gathered her brood together and shielded them behind a window curtain she kept tightly closed. The men on the beach were still slack-jawed when, as they stood immobile in shock, the Brushett house returned on another wave—intact, its curtains still pulled together, displaying Carrie's usual neat housekeeping. Then, plop! The rush of seawater plunked it on the beach a hundred yards in front of them. Their chests heaved great sighs of relief when they heard Carrie's cries for help and the wails of her youngest. Ben bolted and ran to the nearest house for a ladder; he knew the first floor would be full of frigid water and that they'd be on the second floor.

*

The men had also watched the first great wave snatch the Kelly home. Vincent Kelly had built the white two-storey home for his bride, Frances, some fifteen years before. It was near the water on a rocky, exposed patch of land. Since then, the Kellys had had four children: Marion, who was thirteen in November, 1929; Curtis, twelve; Dorothy, and the smallest child, Elroy. Like many Burin Peninsula women, Frances kept chickens, eggs being a good source of protein and essential for the cakes that everyone looked forward to at Christmas and for their birthdays; she had six hens in her chicken house.

Like most men in the area, forty-five-year-old Vincent had done well in the shore fishery the past few years. The Kellys were able to buy eight gallons of molasses, which the children loved to spread on the bread their mother made every day. They also had twelve quintals of salt fish stored in their pantry, a barrel of flour, a hogshead of salt, and a quarter barrel of beef, a favourite meat that they didn't get to eat too often. Alongside the house, Vincent had built a barn to store hay—he had plenty cut in 1929—for his few head of cattle in the winter, and the coal he'd got for the coming cold months.

With Vincent's extra earnings from the successful shore fishery of the past few years, Frances had bought another Singer sewing machine. She had two now; one for her and one for her daughters, Marion and Dorothy. Already Marion was becoming an accomplished seamstress, while Dorothy was eagerly turning her hand to learning the skills from her mother and sister. She was working on pillow cases, a project that would allow her to master straight lines before she tackled more complicated tasks. She looked forward to making dresses like her mother did. Dorothy marvelled when she thought of how Frances had made her own wedding dress. Once in awhile, Frances took her daughters upstairs to her bedroom closet and released the dress from its wrapping and mothballs so that the girls could ooh and aah at it. Frances smiled at their wide eyes; she knew it gave them something to aim for.

Meanwhile, she made sure her family had the finest wardrobe in the harbour; nothing suited a lady better than lovely clothes, as her own mother had told her. Making them was an act of artistry. With the cottons, flannels, and even muslin she collected, she made fine clothes for her children and the sons and daughters of her neighbours in the cove. Little Marjorie Willis, five now, was christened in a white lace gown that Frances had sewn. Ben Hollett's teenage daughters had long, full skirts that Frances made for them. The skirts made their debut at Lady Day in Oderin that August, when the whole bay, Catholic and Protestant alike, gathered to celebrate the feast of the Blessed Virgin Mary and share food, drink, laughter, and stories. Frances had made a Lady Day hat for Martha Cooper, another Kelly's Cove teenager, who had confided to Frances her affection for one of the Oderin boys. Martha had gone into Path End, where she'd bought a straw hat; then Frances sewed layers of violet lace onto the brim. Frances made cotton shirts for the five children of her friend, Carrie Brushett, too; she knew Carrie had her hands full, and for the young son of her neighbours, the Footes. Thus, on Sunday, all the children of Kelly's Cove wore something made by Frances Kelly.

Like Sarah Rennie in Lord's Cove, Frances Kelly had been hard at work with her Singer sewing machine when she felt the rumbling of the earth beneath her. Her foot stopped its almost incessant action on the pedal and she looked up from the machine, fixing her eyes on the kitchen wall opposite. There she saw the kerosene lamp flicker wildly—she lit it at four o'clock every day—and dishes rattle manically. Then she heard the kettle on the stove jump. She creased her brow. She had never experienced anything like this before.

Dorothy had been running her yellow cotton pillow case through the girls' sewing machine. She, too, stopped her work at the sudden eruption of noise and trembling.

"What's that, Mommy?" she asked. She was more curious than afraid.

At first Frances said nothing. She tried to move her mouth but it was as if her tongue was weighed down by sand. She shook her head as if that would clear the odd sensation away. Then she opened her mouth as if to spit out the feeling of sand. "Pphhh!" she said and found some relief with the gesture. Then she turned to her daughter.

"I just don't know what that strange thing is, child," she said. She saw that Dorothy's face was turning red, as if she were holding her breath. "But it can't go on too much longer," she added.

"No, Mommy," Dorothy said. The little girl had stood up when the rumbling started but now she sat down at her sewing machine again. The red drained out of her face and she began to wait patiently, reassured by her mother's words. As the two of them sat there, the dishes, cups and the kettle on the stove continued their odd little jig. The lamp flickered crazily but did not go out.

About five minutes later, the earth became still again. Dorothy and Frances said nothing but let out great gulps of air. It

83

was awhile before they brought their hands back to the cloth and sewing machines.

Frances' older daughter, Marion, was at another house in the village, writing a letter for an old lady who could not write but wanted to send a message to her sister in Boston. Marion wanted to go home when she felt the shock but she stayed put; she would finish the letter and then go—her parents had imbued a strong sense of duty in their children. After Marion signed the old lady's name to the white sheet and folded it, she threw her coat over her shoulders and ran to the Kellys' as if the wind were pushing her.

At the family supper that followed, all the talk was about "the big rumbling," as young Curtis called it. Dorothy could almost laugh about it now that they were altogether—well, most of them; their father, Vincent, had sailed across to the peninsula, his objective to get a full load of wood for the winter. He would be gone for at least a week, probably closer to two weeks. Between his bites of cabbage and fish cakes, Curtis kept making funny noises, imitating the earth and the sounds it had made. It was an earthquake, a neighbour had told him, an earthquake in some far off place. Although they had felt it here in Newfoundland, it was nothing for them to worry about; these things reverberated from quite a distance./

Although she could laugh about it with her brothers and sister, Dorothy still had a bad feeling deep in her belly. Marion felt as if ladybugs were crawling up her chest as she did her English homework at the kitchen table and wrote out the assigned sentence: *"If you do not leave the house, I will send for the policeman with that fine."*

After the children finished their homework, Dorothy washed her long blond hair in the wash basin and, while it was still damp, Marion and Frances tied it in a chaotic pattern of red rags. When it dried, they would free it from the rags and it would be full of "glorious curls," as the magazines promised.

As they finished tying Dorothy's hair, Curtis went out to play. Curtis, who had the energy of a workhorse, begged his mother for another hour or so out of doors before bedtime. The youngest Kelly child, three-year-old Elroy, begged to go with him.

"All right," Frances said to Curtis, finally giving in. "Stay in the meadow on top of the hill near your aunt's house and don't wander into the woods. The fairies are on the lookout for children after dark. But, Elroy, you stay here with us. You're too young yet."

"Take some bread for your pockets, Curtis," said Marion. She was already tearing tiny cubes off the remains of the day's loaf.

"That's right," Frances echoed. "That'll keep you safe from the fairies."

Curtis rolled his eyes. He wanted to be a soldier when he grew up and he wasn't afraid of fairies. "I'm going to play armies," he said. "The fairies will be frightened of me, not the other way around."

"You take it and listen to your sister anyway," his mother said, pushing a red wool cap over his head. "Go on now."

Frances and Dorothy returned to their sewing machines. Curtis barely had time to reach the top of the hill when they heard the roaring of a wave. Marion ran into the yard to see a mountain of a wave slowly approaching them. She scooped Elroy up in her arms and hopped over the fence that separated the Kellys' fence from their neighbours'. When she looked back, her family's house was off its foundation and was just going out to sea.

Gelid salt water had flooded it. The wave lifted Dorothy from her chair and Frances from hers, swallowing them whole. For a minute Dorothy could see her mother's blue dress and white apron. She stretched her hands as far as they could go and kicked her legs in a bid to reach Frances, but then her mother disappeared. Bubbles came out of her mouth, big ones and then small ones. She felt dizzy and she couldn't breath. She had to get to her mother. She'd be safe then. But she couldn't see Frances anymore.

Dorothy kept moving through the water and her head hit something solid. It was the ceiling of the first floor of their house. Oddly, it didn't hurt and she could breath now; she'd reached an air pocket. She gulped huge mouthfuls of air and tried to tread water, like they did in the ponds in summer. For the first time she realized the water was cold and it hit her—this was sea water, not freshwater. *The ocean had rushed into their house.* She shook her head as if doing so would wake her out of a horrible dream. Where was her mother?

She plunged under the water again, looking for the blue and white of her mother's clothing, but everything was grey and dark. And it was moving. The house was moving. The waves had taken the house off its foundation and, Dorothy suddenly realized, hauled it out to sea. She thought of her neighbours on shore; surely they could see this and were putting their boats out to rescue her and her mother. She knew that her father and Vincent Brushett were away, but Billy Foote, Ben Hollett, and a few other men were home. It did not occur to her yet that their houses might be swept away, also.

She pulled her head above the water. The red rags in her hair had come unfurled and had dropped into water like long ribbons of blood. Dorothy began shivering. I must not panic, she thought. She tried to move along the ceiling, trying to find the staircase so she could get to the second storey. It'll be dry upstairs, she reasoned. Maybe Mommy is already up there.

It was hard to move along. The water dragged her down like it was quicksand. Her legs felt like they were made of stone. The lamp had long gone out and the blackness of the night was total now. She didn't know which way to turn. She bit her lip and tried not to cry. Her mother and father would not want her to panic, she reminded herself. They'd want to be proud of her when this is all over. She crept along in the darkness, fighting off a feeling of sleepiness.

"Mommy!" she called out, figuring the shouting might keep her awake and help her rescuers find her.

"Mommy! Where are you? I'm here!"

There was no answer. There was no noise, save the slosh of the waves inside the little house and Dorothy's cries. It seemed now that the house was moving faster, though she didn't know in what direction. Maybe it will be put back in Kelly's Cove, she thought, and all this will be over. But it was as if something was carrying the house a long, long way.

Then the frigid water rose up to the ceiling and Dorothy was covered in it again. Her arms and legs flailed about desperately as she fought off panic. With her hands she hit chairs and table legs and the walls of the family kitchen. Maybe the other houses in Kelly's Cove are gone, too, she thought.

Then she was in the open ocean, just drifting like seaweed. She wasn't cold anymore and, as it enveloped her, the sea began to give a comfort that felt familiar but that she could not recall exactly. The heaviness she had felt in the house had given way and her body was as light as a feather. She lazily opened her eyes and watched lobsters crawl, fish fly by, an eel scoot. It was all so beautiful.

As Dorothy sailed through the waters of the bay, she saw a light that had the brilliance of the finest cut diamond. She floated toward it, overwhelmed by its intensity. All around the light were thick glowing arms that reached for her. They called her name and pulled her to them. Without hesitation, Dorothy fell into their embrace and bathed in their warmth. At once, she felt a love even greater than the great love she had known in her short life as Frances' beloved daughter in Kelly's Cove, Newfoundland.

PART TWO: JOURNEY

12

On the morning of November 19, 1929 the men of High Beach pulled their coat collars tight and pointed their heads to the gale that swept into their village. Just west of Lamaline, their homes faced the French islands, where they often travelled to trade wood and caplin for rum. Theirs was a prosperous community; everyone had at least thirty dollars cash in a jar in their kitchen cupboard, some had as much as $150. A few families had bank accounts with sums of one hundred dollars or more salted away. Their larders were full, as they always were. The Bank Crash was a far off thing that had affected those poor fellows in New York and London, maybe even St. John's, but not anyone here in High Beach.

Thirty-two-year-old Stanley Hillier was one of the men who emerged from his house that morning. He couldn't believe that just yesterday it had been bright, almost spring-like, and the tall grasses in the meadow had been straight as arrows in the still air.

After the great rumbling, his wife, Jessie, had remarked on the glow of the moon on the water. "How lovely it is!" she had said. That afternoon she had stood over the pansies and violas that still bloomed in her garden, their puckish little faces pointed at the azure sky. So small they were, but always the hardiest of her flowers. Still, she noted, she had never seen them make it halfway into November before...

Now Stanley smiled ruefully at the memory of the deceptiveness of the day before. He saw that the pansy heads were drooped, the violas flat under snow. As he walked to the waterfront he met other High Beach men. They were on their way to inspect their property. A few of them had done so after the last wave had receded and they couldn't quite believe their luck, the damage was so minimal compared to what they expected. Now, as the snow flakes thickened, they wanted to be sure they hadn't suffered hallucinations. It was that kind of night, Stanley thought.

When he reached the beach, he stared at the foam of the waves where his stage had been. Only a few broken sticks sloshed against the rocks. His dory was gone, too. He had no idea where it was.

"I found mine inland, in the meadow," old Robert Pittman said, his eyes wide as he pointed to a large clearing behind the small collection of houses that made up the tiny village. "She was tossed there, the first wave, I think. She was thrown so far in the second wave never picked her up."

"Is she hurt?" Stanley asked.

"Not much," Robert smiled this time. "Just needs a little care, that's all. And to be hauled back here."

"We'll do that shortly," John Purchase said. Like Stanley's, his stage had been swept away. Four stages were gone altogether, as were two dories. But every store remained standing, as did every house in High Beach. If the wave had a kind face, it showed it here. Stanley thought of the thousand-dollar life insurance policy he had and counted himself lucky.

Jessie Hillier and the other women of High Beach had begun packing pickled cabbage, bottled rabbit, and tea buns for the men to take to their neighbours in Lamaline. Jessie was worried about them, she had kin there and elsewhere along the coast and no immediate way of knowing how they were.

"You take William Pittman and go over there," she suggested to her husband. "As soon as there's a break in the weather. I'm afraid they're worse off than we are here."

Stanley nodded.

"I'm inclined to agree," he answered. "I wonder if they all got up to the high ground. I wonder if there was any loss of life. God, I hope not."

"And those poor people in Taylor's Bay," Jessie said, pouring her umpteenth cup of tea. "Them on the flattest of land. And Point au Gaul. You know those waves had to take some of them."

"We'll go as soon as we can," Stanley said.

"I hope the food will be some comfort to them," Jessie said. "And if they need more, we got plenty of it. This was a great year for cabbage. I got all kinds of it in the store. Everyone does. Some people got dozens of heads of it—more than they know what to do with."

In the fall of 1928, Dorothy Cherry left her native England to nurse in Lamaline. She was recruited by the recently established Newfoundland Outport Nursing and Industrial Association, more commonly known as Nonia. Nonia recruited nurses for their leadership skills and ability to work independently of physicians, since most of the regions they were going to lacked doctors. They had to be quick-thinking and devoted to duty. Nonia also insisted that they exhibit "missionary zeal" of the Christian variety.

Nurse Cherry met the requirements. ✓

She came from Bolton, in the grey northwestern corner of England. The city of almost 200,000 was only ten miles from Manchester but, like most English, people in Bolton regarded this as a substantial distance and few ever went there. There was no need to, really, for Bolton itself had everything you needed. Straddling the wet and wild Lancashire moors, Bolton grew up as a cotton manufacturing city. It was one of the leaders of the Industrial Revolution, especially when the railway came, linking it to the other smokestack sites in the north and the rest of the country. There had been mills here, too, and mining, but these were beginning their dying days even in Dorothy Cherry's youth. Bolton's boom time was in the ninetenth century—everybody knew that, though no one wanted to admit it. The last great thing that happened in Bolton, Dorothy's father often said over their Sunday roast beef and Yorkshire pudding, was the creation of the Bolton Wanderers, the city's soccer team, in 1888. Seeing them play was just fantastic, the highlight of Dorothy's childhood.

Much of the rest of it was darkened by the cries of Bolton women who had lost their husbands and sons in the Boer War. Dorothy was only a child with a tiny Union Jack flag someone had placed in her hand when the soldiers marched off. She waved her flag and shouted "Hurrah" because everyone else on the street did, but she didn't understand why.

Dorothy was a married woman by the time the next great tragedy happened. Her husband Lloyd was over there, in the trenches with the other Bolton men, fighting "the war to end all wars." It was October 26, 1917 and, like most young wartime brides, Dorothy lived with her parents. Her younger sisters were looking forward to Guy Fawkes Night in a couple of weeks. They would collect pennies for the dummy and have a big bonfire. That afternoon Dorothy entered the crowded post office and heard the postmistress say, "Oh, the most awful thing..." The nurse-in-training looked at the other customers and waited for more. "There's been a lot of our men killed in battle," someone spoke up. Women let out loud sobs and old men looked at each other bewildered. No one moved. Dorothy thought of Lloyd and wanted a cup of tea.

Hundreds of men from Bolton, almost all of them volunteers, had died in the Second Battle of Passchendaele. Members of the Loyal North Lancashire Regiment, they had trained for three years for this battle, which lasted just a few minutes. The two Bolton battalions were on the front line trenches with mud that came up to their waists and was almost liquid. They could not advance properly under these conditions and almost immediately all their officers became casualties. In the end, thirteen officers and 173 men from the two Bolton battalions were killed, with hundreds more wounded. Most of the bodies sank in the mud and were never found.

Lloyd Cherry's body was among them.

After Lloyd's death, the war seemed interminable. It was there when Dorothy baked a cake for her little sister, when her father carved the roast beef at Christmas dinner, when she went to her grandmother's for a summer holiday. Her ears were numb now when she heard "Harry Calderley, you know, from Seattle

Street, he's been killed," or "poor David Knott's mum's got the bad news today. He used to work at Hulton Colliery, remember? She's in an awful state, his mum..." Dorothy tried to drink her tea. That's what they all tried to do. That was the way of the Northern English. What could you do but just get on with it? As Granny always said to her, "Enjoy the flowers while they're out and the rest of the time, just make the best of it." By the time the war ended, more than 2,500 people from Bolton were dead.

Dorothy had come to Lamaline in January of 1929 when snow was general, carpeting the marshes and the beaches with a white still-ness that held God's presence. She had never been outside England; she hadn't been much beyond Bolton and the Royal Bolton Infirmary where she trained, so she hadn't really known what to expect, but she felt ready for anything. And now she was delighted at what she saw. In a rare unguarded moment, she let herself fill with the peacefulness of it; it was a welcome change from the smoky air and street noise of Bolton, she thought. Like all the nurses, she had signed a two year contract with Nonia. Now as she unpacked her belongings, she wondered if her life here would ever get busy. She certainly hoped so, she murmured, letting the peacefulness evaporate; above all, she wanted to be useful.

Then, on the night of November 18, Nurse Cherry found herself in the Catholic church in Lamaline, on the high ground with most of the local people trying to make sense of what was happening. After the first wave people continued to stream into the church, drawn to the fire that was kindled. There they peeled off their clothes, leaden with salt water, and tried to dry them. The paleness of their faces bespoke their terror. Young girls shrieked and children cried in confusion.

Nurse Cherry nodded at each group that entered the church. Her steel grey eyes looked them up and down, taking in every detail. She looked for glassiness in their eyes, for stillness and silence, for anything that would betray shock. She gave only the briefest of looks to those who howled and sobbed. They'll be all right, she thought—they're letting it out. She looked at the men and the boys who were almost men. Keeping it all in, most of them, she thought. But it'll come out later, in a drunken rage in the spring after a trip to St. Pierre, or a heart attack in twenty years time. Thank God they weren't all like that. She gave no thought to herself and which group she was like. She only observed.

Hannah Lake came in with her skirts dragging on the floor with sea water.

"Get them off," Nurse Cherry ordered. "And whatever else is wet."

"How can I do that?" Hannah asked, shifting two-year-old Leslie on her hip. "I've got nothing else to put on." She turned her head to indicate that there were men in the room.

"Hannah, there are women on the way with blankets," Nurse Cherry said. "You get out of those wet clothes the minute they get here. In the meantime, you get up by that fire and get your boots and stockings off. I don't care who sees your legs, lovely though they may be. All your little ones need is a mum with pneumonia going into winter."

"Yes, ma'am," Hannah answered.

"Good girl," Nurse Cherry said. Then she turned to the next arrivals. "What have we got here now?"

*

After the second wave hit Lamaline, a great rush of people scurried up the hill to the church. One of them was a woman whose screams rose to the heavens. She had been one of a group of people trapped on one end of Lamaline between the great waves. They had been trying to get into a dory that was already stuffed with twenty people. They saw this as their only hope of escape from a third wave that they knew was coming, and did. Getting into the dory, the woman tried to carry a kerosene lamp with her and it spilled onto her forearms, severely burning both of them. She then fell into the frigid sea water and somehow waded to safety, followed by some of those who had been in the small boat. Then they ran up the hill, away from the wall of water that was heading for Lamaline.

Now Nurse Cherry ordered men to fetch a bucket of cold water as fast as they could. As soon as the men laid it on the church floor in front of her, she pulled the woman's arms into it. The great cries that followed sent children to their mothers' skirts, their hands clapped tightly over their ears.

"Hold her there," Nurse Cherry told the two men who happened to be closest. "Never mind the screams. Go on."

Then she set to work rooting salve out of her black bag and preparing a dressing. She knew she had Demerol, too, and she would give the victim a shot of that to ease her terrible pain when her charred skin had been soaked enough.

When the people left the church and the others left the Orange Hall where they had gathered for the uneaten supper, two men rowed Nurse Cherry over to nearby Allan's Island. They waited until nearly midnight, when they were certain the seas were angry no more. As they hauled the boat onto shore, a group of women were waiting.

"Nurse Cherry, come to Mrs. Lockyer's, quick!" they said.

Inside on the kitchen day bed was eighty-two-year-old James Lockyer. His seventy-five-year-old wife, Monica, stood over him.

"We had twenty dozen heads of cabbage and it's all gone," she said.

"She's going foolish," someone whispered to Nurse Cherry.

"She's in shock, that's all," Nurse Cherry answered. "Mrs. Lockyer, please sit down and this lady here will get you a cup of tea. I'll see what I can do for Mr. Lockyer here."

As a young woman led Monica to an old pine chair at the table, Nurse Cherry pressed her stethoscope to James' chest. His heartbeat came slowly and reluctantly. It was irregular, too. She opened his eyes and moved her long fingers in front of them but the old man's stare did not waver. Nurse Cherry ran her hands down his arms, legs, and trunk. He's broken most of his ribs, she thought.

"Tell me again what happened to him," she said to the small crowd in the room.

"Our fence is down, too," Monica offered.

Nurse Cherry smiled kindly at her.

"Well, ma'am, the first wave shifted his store," someone said. "Pushed it up toward his house and he got caught between the two of them."

He's been crushed then, Nurse Cherry realized. Probably has massive internal injuries.

"Is there anything you can do, Nurse?" a young woman asked.

"Is he still alive?" said another.

"Yes..." Nurse Cherry began.

"Is he going to live?"

"Well, he's in no pain," Nurse Cherry said quietly. "People in his state can't feel anything."

"What do you mean?" asked the young woman, her face blackening. "What's his state? What's..."

"I mean," said Nurse Cherry. "I mean, he's between this world and the next. I'm very sorry—I can't do anything for him."

The girl stared hard at her, her young face a mixture of anger and pain. Monica's eyes narrowed quizzically. She looked as though she might say something but her lips stayed pressed together.

"He's going to die," another woman said. "There's nothing anyone can do about it."

"Well," said a little girl with curly black hair. "There's something we can do. We can pray."

13

As the High Beach men set out for Lamaline the morning after the *tsunami*, Nurse Dorothy Cherry began her journey by horseback to Taylor's Bay. East of Lamaline, Taylor's Bay lies open-mouthed to the Atlantic Ocean. It first appears on French maps from 1744, where it is identified as *Baue de Tailleur*. For many years afterwards it was frequented by French fishermen on a seasonal basis.

By 1881, it had a year-round population of twenty-one, most of whom were adult men. Knowing they couldn't rely solely on the fishery to keep hunger at bay, they cleared twenty-five acres of land, tossing rocks, pushing boulders, and pulling tuckamore off the earth so they could plant potatoes, turnips, carrots, and cabbage. In the meadows that surrounded the bay they put their one horse, seventeen sheep, fourteen cattle, and fourteen milch cows. Ten years later, there were thirty-six people in Taylor's Bay, including more women.

Most of the settlers were nominally Church of England, but when did they ever see a minister? They didn't have a school but one of the women could read well and she gave seven children lessons in her home during the winter. A few years before the tidal wave, Taylor's Bay was home to eighty-two people; the men fished and the women cured fish on a flat beach that was ideal for such an enterprise. The total value of fish products was at an all-time high. The future looked bright for Taylor's Bay.

All that ended on the night of November 18, 1929, with the first of the great waves that rushed in on the low-lying lands of the village. The next morning Nurse Cherry set out just after dawn. Her breath turned into almost imperceptible ice crystals as she mounted Thomas Foote's mare. Thomas, twenty-seven, walked alongside her, carrying a package of warm bread and tea buns his nineteen-year-old wife, Eva, had baked while it was still dark. "For the livyers in Taylor's Bay," Eva had said as she pressed it into her husband's hands. The mare carried Nurse Cherry's kit and a load of blankets. The Footes had been lucky. Thomas had lost only four quintals of fish and a half ton of coal, substantial, to be sure, but nothing compared to the losses of many of his neighbours whose dories, wharves, stages, and stores were smashed or gone altogether. Albert King, a twenty-three-year-old bachelor, followed Thomas and Nurse Cherry on his bay horse. From the East Side of Lamaline, he, too, had fared comparatively well last night, losing only some fishing gear. He'd have to make it up before the fishing started next spring, but he went to bed counting his lucky stars; things could have been much worse.

Nurse Cherry had an inkling that Lamaline was better situated than some of the neighbouring villages to withstand a *tsunami*. She had often been to Point au Gaul and Taylor's Bay to deliver babies and diagnose bronchitis and even the dreaded tuberculosis. But it was Albert and Thomas who came to her last night and impressed upon her how vulnerable to strong waves these settlements really were. She gulped as she listened to them.

"Then we must go there," she said.

"Yes, Nurse Cherry," Thomas said. "First thing in the morning."

"We'll come by with the horses around dawn," Albert said, sealing their plans. In the meantime, Eva Foote had gone from house to house gathering whatever blankets she could, just in case any houses had been swept away. Now Albert's old horse was loaded down with them, too.

Nurse Cherry licked the snow flakes as they travelled, reminiscent of a game she had played with her brothers and sisters when it snowed back home in the northwest of England. The snow had so rarely stayed on the ground there. It seemed only to come in whispers, like a romance. Here it was as heavy as stew and so thick that it seemed to block the rest of the world out. Already she could see that these little flakes would cling to the gelid ground and lay there till the earth began to warm many months from now.

As they walked the road from Lamaline to Point au Gaul, the little group found long splinters—from wharves and flakes that the waves had broken. They came across shards of butter-coloured pottery and sliced heads of cabbage.

"It's as if God had a temper tantrum," Thomas said.

Nurse Cherry laughed, but he was right, there was so much destruction. As the wet snow thickened, the ground turned slushy and the horses' hooves fought with it. The travelling was so difficult Nurse Cherry thought she'd get seasick on Thomas' mare. Her stomach turned even more and she couldn't get it to stop when she thought of the Bolton men in the muddy trenches at Passchendaele.

"I'll walk!" she said finally. It was slow going and the wind stung their necks as their scarves blew and exposed bits of skin. As they reached the top of the hill alongside Point au Gaul, Nurse Cherry said, "From what you've told me, I think we ought to go on to Taylor's Bay first. I'm quite worried about the people there."

Albert and Thomas nodded their assent. She was a quick learner, their English nurse. Albert stared at her, all eyes ahead under her scarf. How old was she? She seemed middle-aged to him, though she couldn't have been much more than thirty-five.

The trio halted abruptly when they finally reached Taylor's Bay. The whole village was now one sweep of ocean. Where there had been a necklace of stages, flakes and boats around the harbour, there was nothing. There was not even a harbour. All the waterfront property was gone. Even worse, so were most of the houses.

Thomas tried to picture them where they should have been. One side of the harbour was known as the Bonnell side, while the other was called the Hillier side. Jacob and Julia Bonnell's house should be there, he thought. Gus and Dina Hillier's should be over there. The houses must have been swept away. Where were Jacob and Julia, Gus and Dina? And their children? Were they all dead? He had known it was going to be bad, but now his stomach flopped and he struggled against the retching.

Albert's breathing had grown heavy and loud. His eyes scanned the horizon for any sign of the missing houses. But instead he saw boulders, strewn all around the meadows. Some of them looked like they had come up from the bottom of the sea. Boats and fragments of stages lay scattered around. There were no people. My God, I hope they're not all dead, he thought.

Nurse Cherry stole a look at the young men by her side and paled. This was bad. The sea water seemed to be high, or maybe it was just that there were no stages and flakes in the harbour, and, in a sight she never thought she'd see, no boats afloat in a Newfoundland village. Something was really wrong here in Taylor's Bay. Something in her chest hardened.

"Dear me," she said. "Shall we get to work, boys?"

Albert and Thomas were like statues coming to life.

"Look at that," Albert said. "The saltwater comes right into the pond."

The Bonnell side of Taylor's Bay was a disaster. A collection of dwellings looked like they had been hit by heavy shellfire, thought Nurse Cherry. She remembered the bombs that had hit Bolton in 1916. A gigantic German airship had dropped five bombs on Kirk and John Streets, destroying six terraced houses and killing thirteen people. Even a horse was killed, Dorothy had realized in horror. The sounds of fire trucks had filled the air all day and night as the airship kept going, dropping more bombs on Washington Street and the Co-op Laundry on Back Deane Road. Would it hit them next... Nurse Cherry shook her head and fixed her eyes on the sight in front of her. The small party knocked on the door of a house that remained standing and then entered. It was the home of William and Catherine Bonnell, a couple in their twenties with four young children. Nurse Cherry's nose wrinkled at the smell that greeted her. Then she saw a calf and six sheep in the kitchen.

"There's nowhere else for them, Nurse Cherry," said William. "The waves were so high they blotted out the stars."

As soon as he spoke, the nurse's ears tuned into a loud, erratic rattle.

"Who's sick?" she asked.

"It's Catherine, my wife," William answered. "And John, our second youngest. Both of them had a cold and they got fierce wet last night. Now they're real sick."

Nurse Cherry noted the dampness of the linoleum floor and the hooked mats. The house must have been flooded, she thought. She instructed William to remove the damp mats. Then she bent down and folded up the one at her heels and tossed it outside. William followed suit, assisted by the Lamaline men.

"My store is gone," William said as he worked. "And all our potatoes."

"Leave some of the bread here for Mrs. Bonnell, Albert," Nurse Cherry said. She dug her fingernails into her palms as she realized how little food they had brought. There seemed to be people all around her. Besides William, Catherine, and their four children, William's parents and his two siblings were staying in the little house, along with the animals. With William's waterfront property gone, the animals were the only bit of potential income the family had, Nurse Cherry knew. Thankfully, he still had forty dollars in his pocket. But the money didn't mean much now. The Bonnells' inside clothing had been ruined by seawater and there was no merchant nearby.

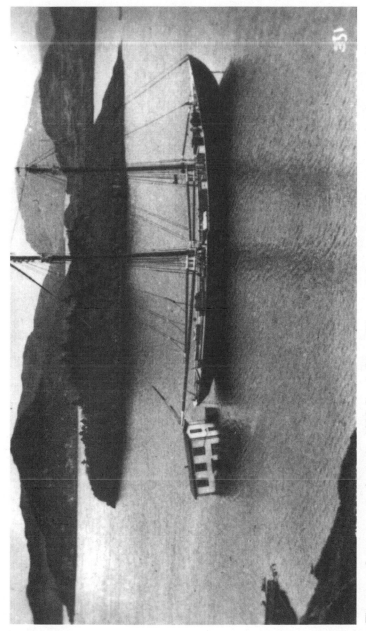

The most famous scene from the 1929 South Coast Disaster. A house washed out to sea by the *tsunami* is retrieved by a schooner. (Centre for Newfoundland Studies Archives)

Waterfront debris. Sticks, staves, posts, cribbing and a wharf platform, left behind in the wave of the *tsunami*. (Centre for Newfoundland Studies Archives)

A house moved off its foundation and deposited at the water's edge, Burin North. This one could be salvaged. (Centre for Newfoundland Studies Archives)

Lord's Cove. From an "H.M.M." postcard found in the Trinity Museum, Trinity Bay. (Photo: Gladys Bonnell)

Dozens of houses were washed out to sea. Miraculously, some survived intact, but most, like this one, were totally destroyed. (Centre for Newfoundland Studies Archives)

West side of Taylor's Bay. From an "H.M.M." postcard found in the Trinity Museum, Trinity Bay. (Photo: Gladys Bonnell)

The graveyard at Lord's Cove. Crosses mark the graves of Sarah Rennie and her three children, trapped and drowned in their sea-level house. (Photo: Garry Cranford)

Burin. The site where Bartlett's Shop once stood. The *tsunami* lifted it off the foundation and transported it to another location. (Centre for Newfoundland Studies Archives)

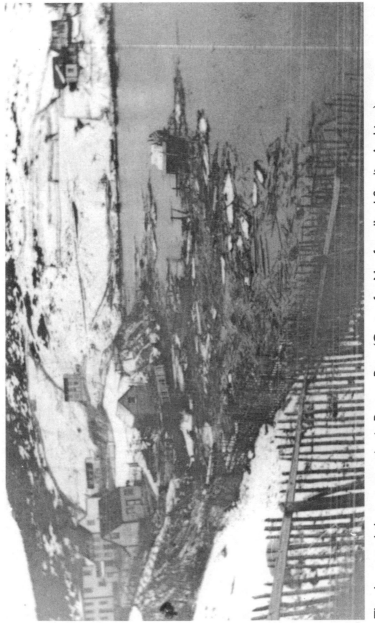

The devastated shore properties in Port au Bras. (Centre for Newfoundland Studies Archives)

At sea, the energy in the waves of the *tsunami* passed unnoticed under ships. In shallow water, however, the energy intensified and vessels were at the mercy of troughs and crests of harbour waves. (Centre for Newfoundland Studies Archives)

Burin Relief collection vehicle. When news of the South Coast Disaster reached the outside world, a committee based in St. John's coordinated the campaign to collect cash and materials to rebuild the fifty communities affected. (Centre for Newfoundland Studies Archives)

Lucy and Malcolm Hollett, 1962. A magistrate at Burin in 1929, Malcolm Hollett coordinated and administered the relief efforts, inventorying the damage, and distributing the relief to those in need. (Photo: Grace Hollett.)

Left: Nurse Dorothy Cherry on the steps of Markland Cottage Hospital. Nurse Cherry received commendations for risking life and limb in travelling from town to town on the Burin Peninsula, giving medical aid to victims of the *tsunami*. With her is a nursing colleague, Bessie Sellars.

Meanwhile, Nurse Cherry wanted to make sure Catherine and young John were kept warm and dry. She examined mother and child, both saucer-eyed and weak. She peeled two blankets off the pile Albert had brought inside the house.

"Heat up a large beach rock or a brick," she told William. "I'm going to wrap Catherine and John in these. They're to stay in them, away from the rest of the family. They've both got bronchitis and you don't want anyone else to get it. They're to stay warm and dry as best they can. There's to be no smoking in the house, and no woodsmoke either."

Then she turned to William's mother, sixty-eight-year-old Jane Bonnell.

"Have you got any wild cherry for an infusion, a tea?" She asked.

Jane shook her head. "You know I got nothing, Nurse."

Nurse Cherry frowned. Bronchitis could kill a small child under these conditions.

"But I'll see if anyone else has something," Jane added. "Some of them still have their houses standing. Well, a few do anyway."

Nurse Cherry smiled and closed her bag. There was nothing else she could do here. She cursed the helplessness that she had always regarded as her enemy.

14

Nurse Cherry swallowed hard many times that day. She forgot to eat as she went from one remaining house to another, even neglecting to get herself a cup of tea. She did her best to reset a seventy-two-year-old man's ankle, though bone setting was never her favourite aspect of nursing. She listened as the man's wife, Martha, talked of her six drowned hens and her root crops all washed away. Martha's predicament was a mean one; her losses meant hungry months ahead and no apparent way around it. The boot of the Burin Peninsula wasn't like Bolton, Nurse Cherry reflected, where you could pop down to Spencer's green grocers on the High Street and buy a head of lettuce or a bunch of carrots.

Also on the Hillier, and less affected, side of the harbour, Nurse Cherry treated an entire family for exposure. Kenneth and Amelia Hillier barely got their four children—Lancelot, Louis, Laura, and baby Leslie—to safety as the waves rushed in. On the way out the door, Kenneth grabbed fifty dollars in cash that Amelia kept in a jar on a high shelf in the kitchen. At the time, he feared it was all the family would be left with.

Now, as Nurse Cherry examined each child in turn, Kenneth explained how, like everyone else, they lost their stage, landing slip, and wharf, as well as his dory.

"How is he going to fish?" Amelia cried out, her eyes wide. She hadn't slept with worry since the waves had taken her husband's boat.

The children shivered as their mother listed off the food that the *tsunami* stole: no less than five barrels of potatoes, three barrels of turnips, three barrels of flour, and a half barrel of salmon.

"There's barely enough flour left in the barrel to make three loaves of bread with," she said frantically. "I can't feed them." Her arms waved wildly at her children.

"And we got no coal left either," Kenneth said. "And we're among the lucky ones in this harbour. Our children are safe and our house is still standing."

With the two Lamaline men standing like sentries in the Hilliers' doorway, Nurse Cherry stood to face the couple.

"The immediate problem is that every one of you is suffering from exposure," she said. "Now, my fear is that it could turn into something worse if you're not careful, especially with the little ones."

She paused while a dark silence descended in the room.

"You must keep giving the children hot tea and give baby Leslie warm water. This is very important. They're cold to the bone and we must warm them up from the inside out. You see how drowsy Laura is? That's not a good sign. So keep pouring hot

121

tea into her. Don't give any of them hot toddies or anything alcoholic, that'd be very bad for them. Cover them in blankets and heat up some bricks or large beach rocks and put them in the blankets with the children. They should warm up with a little time. I know you're fretting about the future, but turn to the children now, and take care of their exposure."

Amelia began gathering her little flock to her. They were dressed in their inside clothes in a frigid house, covered only by sweaters. She would take Nurse Cherry's advice, Dorothy could see that. She needed only to be pulled out of the shock that shrouded her. The nurse moved to the stove and began boiling the kettle. She would start them off before moving on.

"Can one of you men fetch a few beach rocks that we can heat for the children?" she asked. Albert nodded and disappeared through the doorway. Nurse Cherry's eyes scanned the house for blankets. Amelia knew what she was looking for and she ran upstairs to get them. Together, she and Nurse Cherry peeled the woollen sweaters off young Lancelot, Louis, and Laura. Nurse Cherry held baby Leslie close to her, rubbing the child's pale skin to warm it up. Meanwhile, the kettle started to boil and Albert returned with an armload of beach rocks.

"Thank you," the young mother said. "We'll make sure they won't get sick. I'll get the hot water into them right away."

Her husband, Kenneth, pulled a roll of bills out of his pants pocket and handed five dollars to Nurse Cherry. The nurse shook her head.

"I've no need of it," she said. "Give it to one of your neighbours."

*

As Nurse Cherry, Albert, and Thomas walked through Taylor's Bay, they trod over clapboard, shards of glass, scraps of felt from roofs, and torn children's clothing. They shuddered at each new find. The head of a doll sent Thomas jumping again as the face of his own little girl appeared before him.

He gagged again when the trio entered the small home of twenty-four-year-old Hannah Bonnell, her husband, Leo, and their two little girls, Louisa and Ellen. One of the waves had dented the house, but it still stood. Now it sheltered fourteen Bonnells made homeless by the *tsunami*.

The unmistakable sound of a woman's sobbing reached Nurse Cherry's ear as Hannah Bonnell showed them into the kitchen. Elizabeth Bonnell clutched her daughter, Bessie, to her chest, so tightly that the nurse feared for the girl. Elizabeth's cries were as primal as those of a screech owl in the middle of the night.

Her twenty-seven-year-old husband, Bertram, paced across the damp floor, his quick feet making the only other sound in the hushed room. His eyes were dark brown and wide, unblinking as he stared at a distant point. In his arms were two stiff little bodies. He held them as tightly as his wife held their daughter. But Nurse Cherry could see they were as lifeless as two birch junks. Her heart swelled for the man.

In the face of such grief, Albert and Thomas felt like intruders rather than escorts and looked at the floor. Also in the room stood Bertram's parents, whose house had also been swept away, and their four other children. Herbert and Ellen Bonnell were here, too, with their three young children. Their one storey, two room house had been destroyed; like the other Bonnells, they had absolutely nothing left. Now there was nowhere to move in Hannah's packed little house.

As Nurse Cherry looked at Bertram's ceaseless pacing, trying to think what to do, Hannah said of the dead children, "Their names were John, called after his brother, and Clayton."

At that, the boys' mother let out another wail.

The little bodies were dressed in their winter clothes, with woolen caps on their heads and mittens covering their blue hands. The nurse wondered if they might have survived if they'd had less clothes on. She had no idea of the fate of the Hipditch children of Point au Gaul, who had drowned in their pajamas, or the Rennie children of Lord's Cove, who died in their day wear when the first wave crashed into their home.

Dorothy Cherry spoke directly to Hannah.

"Has someone told Bertram the children are dead?" she asked.

"Oh, yes," Hannah answered quietly, releasing a sigh. "He knows they're dead but he can't accept it yet. We think he'll accept it if we just give him a bit of time."

The English nurse reflected on their wisdom. There's nothing I can do for him, she thought. It's his kin who will help him, not me. She remembered how one of her teachers at the Infirmary had told her that part of being a good nurse is knowing when to step back. For the first time, she realized that this wasn't the same as helplessness.

Suddenly there was a thud. Bertram had accidentally dropped one of the stiff little bodies onto the floor. He sank to his knees and laid the other child beside his brother. Then he prostrated himself and sobbed. His brothers and sisters surrounded him, placing their hands on his shoulders, back, legs.

As Nurse Cherry moved toward the door to leave, Hannah stopped her.

"Have you got any food?" she asked quickly. "We're famished and we've got nothing."

The nurse handed her a jar of pickled cabbage, all they had left after many hours in the stricken village.

"I'm sorry," Nurse Cherry said, but Hannah had already turned away and was opening it.

Sidney and Deborah Woodland were among the few whose houses remained standing. Set back from the harbour, their little dwelling was entirely unaffected by the waves. Sidney's biggest problem was facing an upcoming spring with no stage, dory, moorings, or lines. But, as he took in the sight that daylight brought on November 19, he was grateful for all that he did have.

Now the Woodlands' house, home to their own five children, was filled with no less than thirty-two homeless people. They were crammed into the low-ceilinged kitchen, where a dozen children sat on the floor and an old lady slept on the day bed. In the two bedrooms, rows of people perched on the beds, their eyes looking at nothing. The little parlour was blocked with still more of their traumatized neighbours. Goodness, thought Nurse Cherry, if just one of them gets the flu... She realized that they had lost all their winter clothing and could not go outdoors. In most cases, their indoor clothing, too, had been drenched by sea water and had dried out while still on their backs through the dark hours of November 18.

Among the Woodlands' boarders was thirty-five-year-old Robert Bonnell whose wife, Bridget, had drowned the night before. Bridget, whom Robert had courted from Lord's Cove, had been mother to seven-year-old Gilbert, four-year-old Alice, and Cyrus, a toddler. The child she had carried in her arms had been swept away, too. Now, his face buried in his hands, Robert was mad with grief.

Albert and Thomas, the Lamaline men, turned away from him. They had seen so much tragedy this day, more than they had ever seen in their entire lives. Only minutes before they had learned that another Taylor's Bay couple, George and Jessie Piercey, had lost one of their four children to the waves. Thomas was glad that Eva, his teenage bride, was not with him, though he admonished himself for the twentieth time that day for bringing such a small quantity of food. Albert wished they had brought more blankets.

"We should have brought more horses and men," he muttered to Thomas.

Nurse Cherry had called the Woodlands to her side for a talk.

"What have you got in the way of provisions?" she asked them, her brow furrowed.

Sidney drew his breath in, but Deborah answered before he could.

"We were fortunate, Nurse," she said. "We lost no food. And it was a wonderful year for cabbage, all along the coast, I believe. This was the year of the cabbage. I've got ten dozen heads in the store. I've got three barrels of potatoes, a barrel of turnips, two barrels of flour, I made bread this morning—it was gone in five minutes. I've got a barrel of tea, twenty pounds of pork, and a barrel of salmon. The flour not lasting long is my worst fear."

"There's some fish, too," Sidney added, referring to the three quintals of cod that he would feed to his neighbours now rather than sell.

"We picked a lot of berries, too," Deborah smiled. She pointed to the rows of jam jars in the pantry. "I put up blueberry and partridgeberry jam. And I've got some pickled beets, too."

"It's a relief," Nurse Cherry said. "I don't know how long you'll have to feed everyone. I'm sure the telegraph operators are trying their best to get help from Burin and perhaps even St. John's, but the weather's not the best, as you know."

"The crowd over at Hannah Bonnell's have no food," Thomas piped up. "The poor things are half-starved."

"Yes, that's right," Nurse Cherry nodded. "If you think you can spare anything at all, Deborah, please do. I know you will."

"Of course," the young woman said. "I'll send Sidney over by and by."

"In the meantime, let's make sure everyone keeps drinking hot liquids, even if's just hot water, including the little ones," said the nurse. "I know you'll have to spare the tea along."

"I think I'll just use it 'til it runs out," Deborah said. "No one prefers hot water over hot tea. I think help will be here before we run out of tea."

Nurse Cherry smiled at her optimism and the pink in her cheeks.

"Let's get started," she said. The two women boiled pot after pot of water and made tea. They went from room to room giving the hot mugs to adults and children alike, who drank it greedily.

Maura Hanrahan

Between them, Deborah and Nurse Cherry persuaded Robert Bonnell to drink a few sips between his incessant sobs. His young son, Gilbert, too, had some tea, while his little sister Alice napped on her father's lap.

"You're a brave boy," Nurse Cherry told him, almost coaxing a smile. Then she turned to the still energetic Deborah.

"Keep the house warm but not hot," she said. "Give the children a spoonful of jam twice a day to keep their resistance up. When help comes, people will have to move out of Taylor's Bay. It's a health hazard having this many people in close quarters. If one gets sick, everyone will. I'm very sorry."

Deborah pressed her lips together. During the silence that followed, it seemed as if everyone in the house, even in the other rooms, was waiting for her to speak. When she did she said, "I wonder if Taylor's Bay will ever be the same again?"

15

Nurse Dorothy Cherry spent the night of November 19 drifting in and out of sleep, sitting on one of Deborah Woodland's pine kitchen chairs. Her companions, Thomas and Albert, lay curled up at her feet, part of the human mass that covered the linoleum. Dorothy dreamed of England. She was in her grandmother's garden, rich with July violets and smiling pansies. "Enjoy the flowers while you can," Granny said, her blue eyes sharp and lively. Swifts and swallows glided in and out of her dream, then darted across the garden this way and that, as thick as black flies in the Newfoundland woods. In her chubby childish fingers was a ha'penny with Queen Victoria's image on it. It was one of her favourite things, something she kept in her "precious box" under her bed. But now she threw the coin in the air and caught it as it flopped back down...

"Shush, John!"

"Shush, Margaret! You'll be all right now. Be a good girl and you can have some more jam tomorrow."

Mothers were comforting their children and she was in a black, draughty kitchen in a remote village in Newfoundland and her grandmother was buried in a hill in Farnworth in the southwest of Bolton. She pulled the thin flannel blanket over her shoulders and stretched her back a little. From one of the bedrooms she thought she heard a low rattle, a signal that someone had the beginnings of bronchitis. "Oh no," she muttered. Again she cursed the helplessness that dogged her. She wondered if the quake and the fierce waves that came after it had affected the telegraph wires. Goodness, she hoped not. If the cables were broken, there would be delays in getting messages out. This, of course, would postpone the arrival of any ship that might bring much needed medicine, clothing, and lumber to rebuild fallen houses.

As the first light of day began to show, Dorothy Cherry thought of these things and could not fall back to sleep. Besides, Deborah Woodland was up now and fastening her apron around her slim waist. She went into the long pantry and plunged a metal scoop into her flour barrel, emptying the flour into a large bowl. Then she tiptoed back into the kitchen and began the age old task of making bread. This day, too, the comforting smell of rising bread would awaken the mourning people of Taylor's Bay.

The journey to Point au Gaul, which involved backtracking over familiar ground, was made arduous by the frozen mud on the road. Thomas' mare and Albert's bay horse hesitated and then slipped and stumbled over large ridges of earth encased in ice, shaped by the *tsunami* and then the snowstorm of the day before. This time the animals carried no food or blankets; they had all been distributed at Taylor's Bay.

In Point au Gaul, Nurse Cherry ministered to Jessie Hipditch, still prostrate in her sister Nan Hillier's bed, and hysterical with grief over the deaths of all three of her children, Thomas, Henry, and baby Elizabeth. Nan's eyes were rimmed with deep creases, betraying her own lack of sleep as she tended to Jessie. Nurse Cherry ordered Nan to bed and delegated a neighbour to stand in for her at Jessie's bedside, at least for a day.

The nurse sat with Jessie and spoke to her.

"Jessie, do you remember me?" she asked. When there came no answer, she repeated the question, not once but three times above Jessie's babbling. Finally Jessie calmed.

"Yes," she whispered.

"Jessie," Nurse Cherry said, "it's terrible, what's happened. It's so very sad." She stopped while Jessie stared at her, the young woman's eyes great with grief.

"Your little children are all angels in Heaven now, dear," Nurse Cherry continued softly. "You've got to cry for them and then you've got to help your husband, David."

Jessie continued staring at her and then released a new flood of tears. She began to babble again but suddenly stopped and sobbed. Dorothy held her. By now, Nan's eight-year-old daughter, Ruby, had joined them and she sat on the bed and crawled into her aunt's arms. Huge tears slid down Ruby's face.

"I miss my little cousins, Aunt Jessie," she said.

"Oh Ruby!" Jessie cried. "I don't know how I can go on without my babies!"

Jessie sobbed from the bottom of her gut till she flopped back down on her pillow, utterly spent. Her dark hair spread out behind her, damp with tears and sweat. As she fell into a deep sleep, Nurse Cherry stood at the foot of the bed and Jessie's husband, David, tiptoed into the room. He eased in behind Nurse Cherry, saying nothing. Dorothy turned and smiled at him. She noticed the wet shine on his eyelashes.

"I'm so very sorry for your loss," she whispered.

David nodded.

"Will Jessie be all right?" he asked quietly, his eyes full of fear.

Nurse Cherry nodded quickly.

"With time, with a lot of time," she said. "And she has the love of her family. That's so important."

"Will we be able to have more children, Nurse Cherry?" David asked almost in a whisper, his eyes fixed on the floor.

Nurse Cherry smiled and looked at Jessie's sleeping body.

"I think Jessie will want more children, with time. She'll always mourn her lost children, but give her time, David. Don't worry. There's no reason you can't have more children."

David looked at his wife. Then he walked alongside the bed to her side, sat down, and stroked her long hair as she slept.

After a night in Point au Gaul, Nurse Cherry and her escorts travelled to Lord's Cove. By now, they had heard of the miraculous rescue of toddler Margaret Rennie, whose mother, Sarah, had drowned in the family home with three of her children. Margaret had been given up for dead when Lord's Cove men retrieved her from her house, which the first wave had thrown into an inland pond. The whole village had rejoiced when the little girl had awakened after being plunged in a tub of hot water. All along the coast stricken people were taking some comfort from this story.

The road between Point au Gaul and Lord's Cove was all beach now. Instead of earth, it was filled with round grey, blue, and white rocks, smoothed by centuries of wave action, pitched there by the *tsunami*. Albert had borrowed a carriage from a Point au Gaul man and hitched his horse to it, but the animal could not stand the strain of hauling the carriage over the rocks. Before long, Albert unhitched the carriage and abandoned it. Thomas turned around and brought his mare back to Point au Gaul. When he returned to the beach road, he and Albert had to pull the horse over the rocks til they got to Lord's Cove. Although it was a cold November day, sweat ran down their faces and backs.

In Lord's Cove, Nurse Cherry tended to baby Margaret Rennie who, she was glad to see, was in fine shape. Alberta Fitzpatrick had taken great care of her and doted on her. The child kept asking for her mother, though, and she wanted to go home. Her father, Patrick, was in shock, having lost his wife and three children as well as their home. Nurse Cherry was a little worried that the remaining family members were split up, with Patrick staying at one home, his surviving sons, Martin and Albert, with other friends, and little Margaret with the Fitzpatricks. They needed each other now, she worried, but it was hard for a man left on his own with no house. Here again, she would have to give in to that feeling of helplessness and trust in the ways of the people, who certainly seemed to be doing everything possible for the Rennies. Letting go went against her nature, but she had already seen how their wisdom worked.

She reminded herself of this as she tended to a man's crushed finger and treated several lingering cases of shock. At night she went back to Alberta Fitzpatrick's, where people had gathered once again to retell the tale of little Margaret's rescue. They told it like a prayer and as they told it, a much-needed feeling of serenity settled upon them.

16

Albert and Thomas, Nurse Cherry's companions from Lamaline, turned back toward home after a night at Lord's Cove. Thomas was eager to see Eva and their daughter, Mary, and to make sure they were all right after his absence. Albert, too, wanted to see his relatives and ensure they were well. Both men were desperate to see that communications with Burin and St. John's were established and ongoing. Above all, they wanted to alert the telegraph operators to the devastation in Taylor's Bay and the urgent need for provisions of every kind. Nurse Cherry impressed on them that it was necessary to evacuate people from the village lest an epidemic develop.

So it was men from Lord's Cove who accompanied Nurse Cherry on the long journey to Lawn, the next community to the east. The road to Lawn veered away from the sea, so it contained less debris deposited by the tidal wave. But without the moderating influence of the water, the air was cutting and their faces hurt when the wind blew. The horses were irritable and sluggish. The men had to push them to move on. Nurse Cherry again had visions of her grandmother's violets; she wondered why she was thinking so much of them now. And that ha'penny with Queen Victoria's profile on it? She bent her face to the ground and pressed on toward Lawn.

Most of the time she walked since the animals were so contrary. It made the time go faster, too, she reasoned, by giving her something to do. But sometimes she rode on one of them to give her aching legs a rest. When she stopped her calves throbbed and her feet swelled in her boots, so much that she worried if she'd be able to get them off.

The old wooden bridge that led to Lawn was down. The men called across and got some Lawn men to fetch a dory, one of the few that hadn't been smashed to bits. They carried it from the beach to the bridge and then rowed it across the narrow river, breaking the thin ice in places. Then Nurse Cherry got aboard, laughed at her situation, and helped row across. The horses, more unpredictable than ever now, plunged their legs into the frigid water.

"They're spooked by the tidal wave," someone said.

"You'll never be able to predict how they'll act around water now," another added.

At least there are no flattened homes in Lawn, Dorothy Cherry consoled herself as she fell asleep her first night there. And, thankfully, no one had died. She was exhausted; she had travelled at least twenty rough miles and spent another day treating people for shock, exposure, injuries, and even septic inflammations. She was relieved that some who had suffered damage here had substantial savings. Michael Tarrant, who was fifty-six, and his wife, Emma, thirty-six, gave up much of their fishing gear and rooms to the waves, but still had two thousand dollars in the bank. Even young Ernest and Loretta Connors, both thirty, had two hundred dollars saved; now they and their little Gerald would need it, and more. Other families, though, had nothing.

Nurse Cherry was in a bed under a thick quilt this time, her head lying on a pillow stuffed with the feathers of an eider duck. The last thing she saw before the blackness of slumber was a giant violet from far away England. The visions of German bombs dropping on the Co-op Laundry in Bolton had left her in Taylor's Bay. Maybe she had seen the worst of the tidal wave's fury.

The smell of butter smeared on fresh bread drifted into her morning dreams, only to be interrupted by a knock on her door.

"The priest wants you to go to St. Lawrence, Nurse Cherry," said the little girl of the house in as authoritative a voice as she could muster.

Suddenly the cold, fast waters of the tidal wave washed into Dorothy Cherry's memory and she saw the white face of Jessie Hipditch and the arms of Bertram Bonnell, swollen from carrying his dead children. She saw the first wave pull houses from their foundations and throw them inland in a thousand pieces. She saw the second wave haul away from villages, taking houses filled with women and children with it. The wrinkled telegram announcing the regrettable and heroic death of her neighbour, twenty-two-year-old Private Harold Kettle popped in front of her eyes until she squeezed them shut to banish it. She tried to focus on the aroma of the fresh bread but she had to hurry to get to St. Lawrence. She had no idea what awaited her there. She still did not know if the outside world knew what had happened to the people of the boot of the Burin Peninsula. Or if help was on its way. Or when it would or could come. She had no bright news to bring the people of St. Lawrence. Her arms were heavy as she pulled them into her dress. My clothes need a good wash, she thought.

Nurse Cherry's legs ached and swelled as she travelled over the road to St. Lawrence, named centuries ago by Channel Islands fishermen after a Jersey Island parish. Although the town was the largest on the lower part of the peninsula and something of a service centre, life in St. Lawrence still revolved around fishing. Nurse Cherry's little party reached there not long before nightfall, just in time for supper and to administer some basic medicine to a few livyers alongside the priest's house, where she was staying.

As soon as Nurse Cherry finished her breakfast of tea and hard-boiled eggs the next morning, Grace Reeves, a slip of a thing at fourteen, rushed into the priest's kitchen to tell her that "poor Joseph Cusack's house is all destroyed, Nurse." Nurse Cherry let her china cup fall onto her saucer as the maid backed into the dark mahogany doorway to listen to Grace.

"Yes, Nurse," she nodded. "'Tis true, only I forgot to tell you that."

"Oh dear," sighed Nurse Cherry. She knew that Cusack was a widower with three children, the older two in their early teens. Even worse, Joseph suffered badly from high blood pressure. Dorothy swallowed the last of her tea and determined to visit the Cusacks right away. This would not be good for Joseph's health, she knew, and he was all the children had.

She glanced out the window at the snow that was still falling fast. It had been a wild night with the wind emitting war cries hour after hour. Over and over Nurse Cherry woke from the dreams that took her back to the Bolton Wanderers soccer pitch. She was a tiny girl on her father's shoulders, clapping as the Wanderers beat mighty Manchester United. "We're an older team than they are!" her dad called up to her. "You remember that. We've got four years on them." Later that night the Burin Peninsula wind pulled her out of a Wanderers game with Ipswich Town. This time she was even smaller, not yet in school, and it was her first game. The Ipswich players came all the way from southern England—so far away!—her father had showed it to them all on a crinkled old map. Their town was on the Suffolk coast, right across from Holland in Europe! Dorothy's heart beat with excitement as her family went through the gates for the match, surrounded by thousands of other Boltonites. She wondered about the players from Ipswich. Would they look like people in the North or would they be different? She could hardly breathe with... Then the wind pounded on the roof of the rectory, nearly tearing it off, and Nurse Cherry sat up in bed, a mess of confusion.

Nurse Cherry bundled up and faced the gale, with Grace by her side. She found the little family at James Cusack's house, snowdrifts piled high on its side. James was in St. Pierre but his twenty-eight-year-old wife, Elizabeth, was doing her best to tend to Joseph's three children as well as her own brood of four. Joseph had gone to look for whatever building supplies he could find. Nurse Cherry was pleased to hear that he was active and doing something about his situation; pressing on was always the best medicine, she told herself.

"We're the lucky ones," Elizabeth told Nurse Cherry. "We've lost nothing but the breastwork on our wharf. Most in the harbour have lost much more than that."

"There's a great deal of damage in St. Lawrence then?"

"Oh yes!" Elizabeth answered, putting bowls of porridge in front of a row of quiet children. "The businesses are in a terrible state and almost all the wharves are gone. Most have lost food and many have lost boats and coal. I don't know what will happen the winter and next spring when they have to go fishing."

"I suppose I thought it wasn't that bad when most of the houses were still standing," Nurse Cherry said.

"Well, yes, Nurse, you're right there," Elizabeth nodded. "Most of us have our houses and no one died, thanks be to God. I hear that's not the case farther down the peninsula and we've been praying for those people and lighting candles in the church."

"Yes, it's the saddest sight, Taylor's Bay," Nurse Cherry said. "The Bonnell men, Robert and Bertram, losing their children, and Robert losing his wife, too—Bridget, she was from Lord's Cove. Bertram was driven mad with his loss when I saw him. His wife, Bessie, too, she was heartbroken, of course. And then poor Jessie Hipditch and her husband David in Point au Gaul—they lost all their children, all three of them. Jessie's mother, too. And her sister Jemima's daughter, Irene."

The Cusack children stared at Nurse Cherry, trying to take in the gravity of her words. They were catatonic, like statues. Elizabeth was silent.

"I know Jessie Hipditch. I've met her and she's a good woman," she said finally. "It's not nice to lose your mother. But, you know, losing your children is never supposed to happen. It's against nature."

Nurse Cherry nodded. She could understand this. She had delivered many of them and she had closed the eyes of many old people. This was as it should be. In the past few days, everything had been upside down or backwards, just as Elizabeth Cusack had said...

"You'll have to visit poor Michael Fitzpatrick, too," Elizabeth said, as she cleared the dishes off the table and shooed the children away. "His house is gone, too. And his flake and that...Are you all right, Nurse Cherry?"

"Well, I'm a little woozy to be honest," Nurse Cherry answered. Elizabeth paused and looked the nurse up and down.

"Lie down here on the daybed," she said kindly. "Perhaps you've been working too hard or not eating enough or most likely both."

"I've got work to do," Nurse Cherry protested.

"Well, you can't do it right till you rest," Elizabeth said firmly. "Now lie down."

Nurse Cherry moved slowly over to the daybed. Elizabeth pulled a thin woollen blanket over her legs.

"Just have a little rest now," she said gently.

Then one of Joseph Cusack's sons rushed back into the kitchen.

"Aunt Elizabeth!" he said urgently. "There's a rescue ship in the harbour! The SS *Meigle*. Can I go see it?"

"Of course you can, child," Elizabeth said. "Just don't get in the men's way, but offer to help if they need it. Off you go."

Elizabeth smiled when she saw that Nurse Cherry had fallen asleep in spite of her nephew's gleeful news. Her guest woke up only when the dark shadow of a broad-shouldered man standing over her hauled her from the quagmire of her dreams. Two hours had passed when Dr. Mosdell, Chairman of

Newfoundland's Board of Health, appeared in Elizabeth Cusack's kitchen.

As Nurse Cherry blinked her way to clear vision, the doctor introduced himself.

"Nurse Cherry, on behalf of the government of Newfoundland I thank you for your efforts. Now you are coming with us," he said firmly. "We shall take you to Burin on the *Meigle* for a well-deserved rest." He nodded and looked at Elizabeth as if for confirmation. She nodded quickly in return, delighted to be of service. By now the narrow little daybed was surrounded by a gaggle of Cusack children as well as some others who had wandered in to see what was going on. They shook snow all over the linoleum floor as they came in but Elizabeth ignored it, so focussed on Nurse Cherry was she.

Nurse Cherry looked up at Dr. Mosdell and straightened her hair as best she could. "Oh no, I can't go with you—I have work to do, sir," she said weakly.

"Nurse Cherry..." Mosdell began.

"I'm sorry, sir," Nurse Cherry interrupted. "I have to respectfully decline your kind offer."

Two days later Dr. Mosdell dipped his pen in an inkwell and began a letter to the Honourable A. Barnes, the Colonial Secretary in St. John's. He wrote:

> *On board Relief Ship* Meigle *Burin Nov. 25 the Florence Nightingale of the earthquake and tidal wave disaster on the Southwest coast is Nurse D. Cherry of the Nonia Centre at Lamaline. At every point the* Meigle *has called we have heard stirring tales of her courage and*

devotion to the interests of the survivors. Starting her work of mercy immediately after the occurrence of the catastrophe she has known no rest day or night since then and has been without assistance of any kind until the arrival on the coast of the Doctors and Nurses of our relief expedition.

It must have been almost superhuman effort for Nurse Cherry to make her way on foot all through the stricken area from Lamaline to Lawn a distance of twenty miles. Roads and bridges were swept away and she had to wade many of the streams en route. The weather was intensely cold with snow falling all the time. Her ministrations proved nothing less than providential to terror stricken and frightened women and children. She got through the District as quickly as possible sparing herself not at all and after rendering first aid in one settlement she moved on along until something had been done everywhere to help and to cheer the stricken. Courage and devotion were required for the journey which was made right after the woeful destruction of the tidal wave with miles of desolation to be traversed at night and nobody just sure that the catastrophe would not be reenacted.

All day yesterday the Meigle *sheltered at Lawn a Southeast storm with high seas and driving rain rendering communication with the shore almost impossible. Toward evening the rain turned to sleet and there was nothing to do except wait until the dark and tempestuous night had passed. During a lull in the storm of the morning Nurse Cherry was taken onboard. She was almost in a state of collapse after her strenuous and self-sacrificing efforts. Despite her objections the expedition kept her with them and have taken her as far as Burin to enable her to recuperate. She returns to her District by the* Argyle *tomorrow...*

PART THREE: AFTERMATH

17

APPALLING DISASTER ON SOUTH COAST
27 LIVES LOST AND 18 TOWNS AND VILLAGES SWEPT BY
TIDAL WAVES FOLLOWING EATHQUAKE
PROPERTY LOSSES MAY EXCEED MILLION DOLLARS

From the South Coast of Newfoundland comes a tale of tragedy most appalling, following the earthquake of Monday evening 18th. Owing to communications systems having been out of operation by the quake and storms, news of the tragedy was tardy in coming in, and the first intimation of the seriousness of the disaster was conveyed in a message to the Prime Minister from the captain of the S.S. Portia *dated from Cape Race last Thursday, which read as follows: "Burin experienced very severe earth tremors 5:05 pm, tidal wave which swept everything waterfront, 16 dwelling houses with 9 lives mostly women and children gone, 4 bodies recovered. All communication of wire cut off. Report is that 18 lives were lost at Lord's Cove and Lamaline."*

The Western Star

145

Nature showed no mercy to the people of the Burin Peninsula on the morning following the most harrowing event of their lives. November 19, 1929 dawned bitterly cold, and iciness seemed rooted deep in the earth. Soon snow fell, slowly at first and then thick and fast. Before long the villages of the peninsula were enveloped in a cold, cruel, blinding white. The wind howled like an angry husky dog at night, blowing the bodies of dead sheep into the waters of Lord's Cove and Lamaline, and dashing teapots and broken dishes upon the rocks that hugged the shores of Burin and St. Lawrence. Pieces of lace curtain flew on the waves that the post-*tsunami* winds whipped up. If an airplane had been able to defy the winds and fly over the Burin Peninsula, its occupants would have seen clapboard floating like matchsticks and houses bobbing here and there, oddly, as if they were enjoying their sea-going excursion after decades of being anchored to land. Entire harbours were choked with the carcasses of cows, bulls, and goats, and with broken barns, wrecked fences, and dwellings cut in half by waves that had the sharpness of saws.

Meanwhile, wave-battered houses onshore sheltered grey-faced, hollow-eyed people who shivered at the sight of the snowflakes falling from the sky. These people were the homeless. Among their number were Patrick Rennie and his motherless sons of Lord's Cove; David and Jessie Hipditch of Point au Gaul who had lost their three children; William and Carrie Brushett and their children of Kelly's Cove; Vincent Kelly, who had lost his wife, Frances, and daughter, Dorothy, to the tidal wave; the widower, Joseph Cusack, of St. Lawrence; and numerous families in the severely stricken communities of Taylor's Bay in the south and Port au Bras in the north.

146

Tragedy was general on the lower half of the Burin Peninsula following the *tsunami*. So was confusion. The Corner Brook *Western Star* was not unique as it laboured to determine the extent of the damage and loss of life. In the days immediately after the quake the Burin Peninsula was virtually cut off from the rest of the country and the world. In turn, Newfoundland itself was unable to communicate with the outside because of the tidal wave and the damage it wrought. The Bay Roberts Cable Station reported that cable lines between Newfoundland and New York were damaged and inoperable. The cable ships *Lord Kelvin* and *Cyrus Field* located the cable breaks 360 miles south of St. John's. There were twenty-eight breaks in more than 212 oceanic cables near the epicentre of the quake. The French government had its own cables—three in total—and these, too, were broken. Fifty new miles of cable would be required to make the repairs at a cost of $400,000 in 1929 dollars. The French estimated that the repairs would take no less than two years.

Within the country, the main means of transportation was boat. Thus, sea travel and wireless would have to be relied upon to convey information about the effects of the *tsunami* in the towns and villages of the Burin Peninsula. One of those eager to get the message out was George Bartlett, owner of a large general store in the town of Burin. Bartlett's store would go down in legend because of what happened to it on the night of November 18, 1929. The store was housed in a building fifty-five feet by thirty feet, anchored on a concrete foundation. There were no witnesses to the event, but Bartlett's store had turned 180 degrees and travelled two hundred feet that strange night. Amazingly, the building was not destroyed; it landed in a neighbour's yard, right up against their house, completely intact. Even more remarkable was the fact that not one item inside the store, including dishes, lamps, and inkwells, was broken or even disturbed.

Two days later, Bartlett took pen to paper to alert Newfoundland's prime minister of the gravity of the situation facing his neighbours.

Burin North, Nov. 20, 1929
Right Hon. Sir Richard Squires K.C.M.G.,
Prime Minister

Dear Sir:-
This is to acquaint you of a terrible disaster that has overtaken Burin and adjacent settlements, and to appeal to you and your Cabinet to send help quickly. All the waterfront of Great Burin consisting of stores and stages were swept away with all fishing gear and provisions for the winter. Burin proper all the waterfront is damaged more or less I myself have lost considerably but of that I will not mention.

Port au Bras had been cleaned out nothing left standing except a few houses, there has been a loss of seven lives at that place. Foots Cove all waterfront gone with loss of three lives. Rock Harbour has been swept also, I hear also that St. Lawrence is swept clean but as the telegraph lines are down we cannot hear. The S.S. Daisy has gone there and no doubt you will get a full report from them. After the quake a tidal wave of about 15 feet swept this part of the coast and you know what that meant when all stores etc, are only built about five feet above high water line. The conditions are beyond describing as people lost all their coal provisions for the winter, the merchants are in practically the same state and one can hardly help the other. My own nerves are so shaken I can hardly write coherently or legibly as only a person that has gone through such an experience can understand it.

Organized relief should be undertaken as quickly as possible as the winter will soon be on us and hundreds of people have lost their all. As no doubt you will get a full report from Official Circles, you will be able to judge. My object in writing is to stress the urgency of immediate help to the stricken places. Some have no home or any means or getting anything to rebuild and have nothing only what they could catch from the water as they fled from their houses. I know the appeal will not be in vain.

Yours very truly,
(Sgd) George A. Bartlett.

18

Nineteen-year-old Isabel Gibbons was the telegraph operator in Marystown on the Burin Peninsula in November,
1929, when the waves came crashing into the shores. Isabel was
carrying on a family tradition that included her uncle who had
worked with Western Union in New York and her older sister,
Elizabeth, who worked with the same company in Boston. Isabel
came from St. Mary's on the Avalon Peninsula in eastern
Newfoundland, where her paternal grandmother was the first
operator. In turn, Mrs. Gibbons passed on her skills to her son,
Isabel's father, who taught his daughters telegraphy, a valuable
communication tool in those days. Mrs. Gibbons ran the telegraph office in her home. It was no surprise, then, that her four
daughters became telegraph operators, too.

Isabel started work in Marystown, one of the most sheltered
harbours on the Burin Peninsula, in 1927. She lived about a mile
from the telegraph office, which she shared with Eddy Reddy, who

served as the postmaster. They also had a messenger on staff, a young married woman. Isabel worked 9:00 to 6:00 from Monday to Saturday, and 9:00 to 10:00 and 4.00 to 5.00 on Sunday.

Mrs. Forsey, the operator from Grand Bank, was sending messages to St. John's when the Marystown telegraph office pens and inkwells started to rattle on the evening of November 18, 1929.

"What's wrong? What's wrong?" Mrs. Forsey called over the wire.

Isabel stared at the shaking items on her desk. She was awestruck.

"I...I don't know," she answered her colleague in Grand Bank.

"What's gone wrong?" Mrs. Forsey cried again. "Everything is rattling."

"It's rattling here, too," Isabel said. As her voice faded away, the noise grew louder. Then the line snapped and she could hear Mrs. Forsey no more. The office was eerily quiet. Isabel removed her headset and spun around in her chair to face Eddy, who stood behind her, half a dozen envelopes in his hand. He was like a statue.

"The cable between Burin and Marystown is gone," Isabel said calmly, though her heart raced in her chest. She looked down at her hands, shaking on the armrests of her chair. She thought of the others on the line, people she knew so well, although she had never met most of them: operators from Garnish, Fortune, Lamaline, St. Lawrence, Epworth, Burin, Baine Harbour. Everyday she heard everything they said on the lines. They took turns sending messages, each one more patient than the last.

Somehow Isabel could still get through to St. John's. As she realized this, she also noticed that the rumbling and rattling had stopped. She checked the line to Grand Bank but found that it still wasn't working. She would try to reach the capital, though. But then a cable between Terrenceville and Baine Harbour broke and she couldn't reach St. John's. She frowned and looked at Eddy who shrugged, his lips pressed together. Neither spoke. Isabel could not communicate with anyone, but she stayed at her post until closing time at 6:00 p.m.

That night she walked over to nearby Creston with a group of young women. Like Marystown, Creston was protected by Mortier Bay, which separated it from open waters. By now Isabel had heard incredible stories about waves as high as buildings in New York. The women stood at the waterline and watched floating sheds and skiffs ripped from their moorings. They knew that places like Kelly's Cove and Port au Bras were more exposed to the sea and they worried about the damage that might have occurred there.

"I wonder if anyone died?" Isabel said.

"My dad said a score of people have died farther out the bay," one of the young women answered her.

"That's just rumour," said another. "No one knows for sure. And people always exaggerate when the unexpected happens."

Isabel returned to her office the next morning at nine o'clock sharp, rushing to her lines to check for signs of life. There was none and her shoulders slumped in despair. She shook her head at Eddy when he appeared at the door. He sighed in response. Between customers coming in to check on telegraphs and mail, Isabel and Eddy traded stories they had heard about houses swept out to sea and little girls drowned.

When Isabel kept saying it's just rumours at this point, Eddy said, "There was a time before telegraphs, Isabel, and we had to go by each other's word then." Then he stopped while Isabel bowed her head.

"We do know there was terrible loss of life in Port au Bras and that Vince Kelly's wife and daughter are drowned," he added.

Isabel's face reddened.

"I'm sorry, Isabel," he said. "It must be hard on you, being away from your own people at a time like this."

The young woman nodded.

"I wish I knew what was going on," she said quietly.

"That's your way, being a telegraph operator," Eddy said, his mouth turning up. "You're a pro through and through!"

Isabel let out a small laugh through the fogginess that clogged her chest and throat.

She went into her office the next day and the day after, though the lines remained dormant and broken. She stayed until six o'clock every day, listening to the people of Marystown come in and tell what they had seen and heard since the waves had crashed upon the shores of the peninsula. The snowstorm of the nineteenth was followed by a calm on the twentieth, which seemed to offer some small promise that there was something other than chaos in the world.

But by the end of the third day, stories were starting to trickle in from as far away as Lord's Cove and Taylor's Bay. Could it really be true that a woman had lost all her children to the tidal wave? Was a toddler really saved after her mother and siblings had drowned? Isabel wondered and she reflected that her mother often told her there was much that only God could understand.

On the fourth day after the *tsunami*, a messenger arrived from the telegraph office in Epworth near Burin, asking for Isabel to come and assist them. Isabel's eyes brightened at the request and her shoulders cast off a load of which she had not even been aware. It was, she realized, helplessness that had been dogging her. That afternoon, with an overnight bag in her hand, she boarded a small boat to travel to Epworth, sailing out through Mortier Bay, still littered with the odd piece of clapboard or broken stagehead. Isabel wrapped her wool scarf around her face as the boat travelled past the sheltered inlet of Little Bay, then the mouth of Beau Bois harbour and into the winter-like wind. The hollow faces of people made homeless by the tidal wave passed before her as Stepaside and Port au Bras drew near. She uttered a "Hail Mary" for them and tried to focus on the work ahead of her.

Almost unique in the region, the telegraph office at Epworth was capable of receiving and sending messages. In the days following the tidal wave, people from surrounding communities had poured into the Epworth office to communicate with friends and relatives in St. John's and other parts of the country. The operator could not keep up with the volume of messages and was desperate for Isabel's help.

As soon as she landed in Epworth, Isabel went straight to the office and to work. She barely had her coat off when the Epworth operator handed her a stack of messages. "Hello! Thanks!" the bulky woman said breathlessly, and quickly returned to her own pile of papers.

As she laboured in the gathering darkness, Isabel learned what the tidal wave had done to the people of Burin. She knew now they needed lumber for stores, stages, flakes, barrels, furniture, houses, boats—and coffins. They needed coal, clothes, boots, and food. They needed sympathy, consolation, answers. And they needed all these things in a great hurry. Her fingers tapped out their urgency, the flustered heat of her warm blood driving them. As the clock ticked midnight, she finished and fell back in her chair, letting what energy she had left drain out through her legs and feet. Inside Isabel's chest was a black lump made up of the stories she had told through the language of dots and dashes. She took it to a strange bed with her that night in Epworth.

The next morning the local telegraph operator told Isabel the cable between Epworth and Burin had been repaired and that the Burin office could get messages to St. John's. The woman thanked Isabel for her help and arranged her passage back to Marystown. When Isabel left, the black lump was still there.

19

The great gushes of water had reached the shores of the Burin Peninsula on a Monday night. With the telegraph cables broken and Isabel Gibbons and the other operators unable to communicate to sites beyond the afflicted communities, the rest of the world did not know the extent of the damage and pain wrought by the *tsunami*.

On Tuesday night thirty-eight-year-old Magistrate Malcolm Hollett wiped the sweat off his face as he composed yet another letter to Prime Minister Richard Anderson Squires in St. John's. Hollett sat at a mahogany desk in his Burin parlour, feeling no comfort by the smell of century-old oak wall panels or the tray of tea and gingerbread a maid had left for him. He dipped his pen in the inkwell and began again.

> *The SS* Daisy *which was lying at the Government wharf at the time has been rendering every assistance since the affair happened. All Monday night they were*

searching among the houses which went out to sea, for the missing people. All day yesterday in a raging south east gale and heavy sea she was doing the impossible with regard to boats and schooners.

Hollett bit his bottom lip. There was no way to get the letter to St. John's, at least not the last time he sent a messenger to the telegraph officer to check an hour ago. The darn lines were still down and suddenly travel by ship seemed slow. It felt like they were on their own, on the edge of the world, nay, the universe. What an odd position for Newfoundland, a sea-going nation, whose men and ships regularly travelled to Iberia and the Caribbean.

Then his mind jarred back to the tidal wave. Hollett kept writing—he had to do something.

The officers and the crew deserve the greatest effort for the work they have done. Nearly every boat afloat of course was out of commission. I asked the Captain of the Daisy *to go to St. Lawrence and Lamaline today and expect her here tonight. I fear there is great destruction between here and Lamaline. At present all communication is cut off but the operator Mr. Cox is making every effort to establish communication with outlying settlements and with St. John's. I shall endeavour to get some data with regard to the losses and with regard to the distress. It is imperative that something be done at once to relieve the immediate wants of the people who have lost their all. I appeal to you, Sir, for some immediate Government assistance for the people. I shall form a Committee of some of the citizens here in a day or so. In the meantime I shall have to get food, clothing and coal to many families. I hope to send this to you by the* Daisy *to Argentia.*

I have the honour to be,
Sir,
Your obedient servant,
M. Hollett

After signing the letter, Hollett set down his pen and stood up. He walked to the parlour doorway and called out to his wife Lucy, who was on her way upstairs with their baby. "Shall we send Peter back to the telegraph office to see if the lines are working? I've got to get a message to St. John's."

Although the cable lines were still not functioning, Hollett wrote again on Wednesday to the government in the capital. The *Daisy* had brought much sad news upon her return to Burin. This time Hollett reported the death of old Thomas Lockyer of Allan's Island, who had been fatally crushed in the tidal wave. And he sadly recorded the death of Jessie and David Hipditch's three children in Point au Gaul. He had already written of the deaths of Frances Kelly and her daughter, Dorothy, in Kelly's Cove, and the near drowning of the elderly Inkpens from Stepaside.

Now the magistrate's face was permanently the colour of a beet; it had turned that way after the *Daisy*'s Inspector Dee told him that fifteen of twenty-four families in Taylor's Bay were homeless and that the harbour was a wasteland. Of the villages closer to his own home in Burin, he wrote to the prime minister, *"William Moulton's house is washed away. The family barely escaped with their lives... Corbin practically every bit of waterfront property with some dwellings gone."*

After some time alone in his parlour, Hollett made a bold suggestion to the prime minister:

In my opinion this affair is almost too big even for the Government and a general public subscription should be started immediately. It is impossible to describe this dire calamity which has come upon us. I respectfully suggest that an immediate investigation of the individual losses and destitution be made at once on the whole coast concerned. That a boat with provisions and coal be sent as soon as possible, and that a committee be appointed to handle its distribution.

On Thursday morning, three days after the tidal wave, telegraph operators in St. John's reeled in shock when they received the news from the wireless operator on the SS *Portia* calling from Burin. The message was sent to Prime Minister Squires from Magistrate Malcolm Hollett.

SS "PORTIA"
Via Cape Race
Nov. 21, 1929
Sir R.A. Squires,
St. John's.

Burin experienced very severe earth tremors 5.05 PM Eighteenth followed at 7.35 PM by an immense 15 feet tidal wave which swept away everything along waterfront sixteen dwelling houses with nine lives mostly women and children gone four bodies recovered all communications by wire cut off report is that 18 lives have been lost at Lord's Cove and Lamaline S. S. "DAISY" rendering every assistance St. Lawrence also swept no lives lost destruction property terrible and many people left destitute and homeless doing all possible to relieve suffering "DAISY" now at Lamaline writing particulars.

(Sgd) Magistrate Hollett.

*

159

The telegraph operators had seen St. John's harbour empty for a full ten minutes on Monday evening but that was all. It had been a strange sight—a once in a lifetime kind of thing, everyone said—but it had not been followed by anything like the monstrous waves to which the villages of Burin had been subjected. Instead, St. John's harbour had slowly filled with sea water again until it regained its usual fullness. People had even laughed about it. But in the mercantile town of Burin and neighbouring villages, they learned, everything had been destroyed, and most sadly of all, women, men, and children had died. Up to Thursday, the twenty-first, the telegraph operators in the capital knew almost nothing of the tragedies farther south on the peninsula.

Sir Richard Squires, Newfoundland's prime minister, got Hollett's message just before noon. Straight as a flagpole, Squires stood in his office giving dictation. Although he was lean, his little round glasses made him look owlish and academic, though he was neither. He seemed, in fact, to sail from one ill-advised decision and scandal to another. His last term of office had ended under the cloud of corruption charges which were never proven and rumours continued to swirl about him. Anderson, as he was known to friends, also lacked the easy charm of his wife, Lady Helena Strong Squires. Although Helena was the first woman elected to the House of Assembly, she had initially opposed women's suffrage. Now, as a member of the House, she had won many fans.

Squires sank into his overstuffed leather chair as he listened to a messenger read him a telegram from Burin. He crossed his arms in front of his chest as if to ward off what he was hearing.

"My God, it's winter," he muttered. "It's bloody cold out and the fishing's over. And the dead..."

He stood up quickly. He wiped his brow and telephoned Clyde Lake, the Minister of Marine and Fisheries, to inform him of the disaster and to ask him to ready his officials for immediate assistance to the stricken region. Squires then directed the Deputy Minister of Marine and Fisheries, W.P. Rogerson, to contact the railway authorities to commission the SS *Meigle* as a relief ship. He directed his officials to organize a special meeting of Committee of Council, which was also attended by Clyde Lake and Dr. L.E. Keegan, Superintendent of the General Hospital.

Squires emerged from the meeting to send a telegram to Magistrate Hollett:

> AS RESULT MESSAGES RECEIVED FROM YOU AND OTHERS THIS MORNING S.S. *MEIGLE* IS BEING DISPATCHED THIS EVENING WITH MINISTER MARINE AND FISHERIES DOCTORS MOSDELL CAMPBELL AND MURPHY AND MR. FUDGE TWO NURSES MEDICAL SUPPLIES AND PROVISIONS SO THAT WHOLE SITUATION MAY BE FULLY AND EFFECTIVELY HANDLED WITH GREATEST POSSIBLE DISPATCH STOP KINDLY KEEP ME FULLY ADVISED ALSO PLEASE NOTIFY OTHER STRICKEN SETTLEMENTS OF DISPATCH OF RELIEF SHIP.
> RICHARD A. SQUIRES

After the meeting Squires' bureaucrats drew up a list of provisions to be purchased and then had these rushed to the dock in St. John's for shipment on the *Meigle*. Dr. Keegan prepared medical and nursing supplies, while Dr. Mosdell, Chairman of the Board of Health, arranged for doctors and nurses to join the ship to take care of the injured. At this point, the authorities in St. John's could only guess at the scale of injuries and illness brought on by the tidal wave. They knew Magistrate Hollett was not given to exaggeration; there had to be more deaths south of Burin.

In St. John's, everyone involved worked frantically, uttering prayers as they rushed from their offices to the Royal Stores, where they bought most of the goods, to the waterfront. By 8:30 p.m. the *Meigle* was loaded with personnel and provisions. The *Meigle* was built in Scotland in 1886 and weighed 835 tons. Originally called the *Solway*, she was more than 220 feet long. The Reid family, Newfoundland merchants, brought her to the island country in the winter of 1913 and named her after a place near their patriarch's birthplace. They used her as a passenger and cargo vessel. Now, under the ginger-haired Captain Vince Dalton, she would be on a mission like no other.

The ship carried 2,688 four-pound sacks of flour; one hundred barrels of beef; one hundred barrels of pork; two thousand pounds of sugar; 1,020 pounds of tea; two hundred pounds of butter; and four hundred quarter-bags of hard tack. She also carried nails, window glass and putty for house repairs, but no lumber. Captain Vince Dalton, tall and quiet, and his ship pulled away from the finger piers in St. John's harbour at 9:30 p.m. and disappeared beyond the Narrows a few minutes later.

By three-thirty the next afternoon, the *Meigle* was tied up at the wharf in Burin.

Not long after landing, Dr. Mosdell sent a cable to Dr. Barnes in St. John's, describing the *Meigle*'s November 22 arrival:

Shores of Burin Beach strewed with wreckage of all sorts. Houses and stores floating waters of Harbour and dotted along beach partially or wholly submerged. Stages and whurves swept away in almost every Cove and Harbour. Destitution general wherever tidal wave did its work of destruction. Food fuel and clothing badly needed. Stores of food on ship sufficient meet present requirements. Medical and Nursing staff on ship now busy attending number of cases of severe injury and of shock consequent on sudden and tragic nature of disaster.

Hollett was at the front of the crowd that came out to meet the *Meigle*. He pumped Captain Dalton's hand as the skipper jumped onto the wharf.

"Thank you for coming on such short notice," he said, nodding. Then he spoke quickly. "These are the members of our local committee, representing the villages from Rock Harbour to Corbin. Mr. Cheeseman, from Port au Bras... Mr. Lefeuvre, from Bull's Cove... Captain Foote, from Stepaside... Mr. Albert Grant, from Corbin... Reverend Miller... Reverend Hiscock... Reverend Morris..."

Dalton's face registered surprise as he shook hands with each of the men.

"We had to be organized, Captain," Hollett explained. "The tragedy is so great."

Dalton nodded.

"We have twenty homeless families between here and Corbin, sir," said Albert Grant loudly.

Oddly, Dalton found himself feeling guilty at this; he said nothing. Then his first mate stepped up and listed off the food and building supplies that the *Meigle* had brought.

"We're very grateful and will convey this gratitude to Prime Minister Squires and his government," Magistrate Hollett said. The scores of people that surrounded him remained quiet, and for the first time Dalton noticed the dark circles under their eyes. "I fear it will not be enough, though."

"No?" Dalton said, realizing how inadequate he sounded. "My God, did you say there are twenty families homeless?"

"Indeed, I did, Captain," Albert Grant spoke up again. "Indeed I did."

Dalton caught the angry tone in the fisherman's voice again.

"We don't have anywhere near enough supplies to help them," Dalton said as a thumping gathered steam in his chest.

"No, sir, we don't," the first mate echoed.

"We expected that," said Hollett. "Food is more important now, it's our first priority for this area. We've put the homeless families in with other families and that will have to do until other plans can be made."

Dalton nodded slowly. Think, he told himself, think! Slowly he shifted himself out of his catatonia. The disaster was of greater proportions that Squires, Lake, and everyone in St. John's realized, that much was sure. Other ships might have to join the *Meigle*. He thought of his blue-eyed wife, Cora, at home on Old Topsail Road in St. John's; she'd probably be setting out the supper dishes now. Take one step at a time, she'd say.

"You said food is the first priority for this area, Magistrate Hollett," Dalton began. "What are the other priorities?"

"Coal," Hollett answered quickly. "Most families are in desperate need of it, so much of it was swept away, and here we are on the cusp of winter."

"I can purchase coal for you on behalf of the Newfoundland government," Dalton said. "When a ship comes into Burin with coal, let me know."

"There's one here now, sure," someone called out from the crowd.

"There is indeed," said Reverend Miller, a member of Hollet's committee. "The *Newcastle*—perfect."

"I can buy two hundred and fifty tons and your committee can distribute it," said Dalton. "It's not much but it's a start."

Hollett and his colleagues nodded. Dalton noticed that Hollett's frown never went away.

"We appreciate that, Captain. Our other priority is that you get to the southern parts of the peninsula as fast as you can," said the Magistrate. "We've heard that things are really bad in Taylor's Bay and Point au Gaul. We're very worried about those places. They're on flat land and very exposed to the water."

Hollett's face was tight when he finished.

Dalton recalled the villages of which the magistrate spoke. Hollett was right; those little villages and others like them would indeed be particularly vulnerable to the tidal wave of November 18. He wondered what remained of them. He studied Hollett for a moment, seeing the intensity under the magistrate's bushy eyebrows and hooded eyes. He knew the man was learned; Hollett had been Newfoundland's Rhodes Scholar and studied at Oxford University. He was no coward either, Dalton reckoned, recalling that he had served in the Royal Newfoundland Regiment and been seriously wounded by shell-fire in France in 1916 before being invalided back to his home country. If Hollett said things were bad here and farther down the coast, then they probably were.

"We should take as many supplies as we can to those communities," Dalton said. "But you'll need some, too."

"Take three-quarters of the food south of here," Hollett said, meeting the eyes of his fellow committee members. "That's where the need will be greatest."

20

Besides some of the food, Captain Dalton and the *Meigle* left the Burin Committee with three of the physicians on board. Nurses from St. John's accompanied each of the doctors.

Captain Dalton knew that it was impossible for a vessel of the *Meigle*'s size to land at Taylor's Bay and other low lying places at night so he over-nighted in Burin. Early the next morning the *Meigle* left Burin, but as soon as Burin harbour faded into the distance, snow began falling. Very soon, winds blew out of the northeast, quickly encasing the *Meigle* in ice. The cold was jarring. The ship inched through the gelid waters of Placentia Bay, a little tub on an angry November sea that would not quit.

Finally, a full twenty-four hours later, the *Meigle* reached Point au Gaul. Captain Dalton stood on deck and surveyed the harbour. There was not a single wharf standing—nor were there any stages or flakes. The giant waves had destroyed a hundred out-buildings, taking their contents—gear, food, fuel—to the bottom of the sea, or pitching them in a meadow two hundred yards behind the village where they lay in ruins. Over forty boats had been swept away, most of them torn to smithereens.

It took all day but Dalton and his crew lowered food into the *Meigle*'s lifeboats and then landed them to a grateful populace. One of the Point au Gaul men collecting the food onshore was twenty-eight-year-old William Lockyer, a fisherman who had lost his motor dory, stage, and store to the *tsunami*. William and his wife, Rebecca, had got their three little daughters to safety as the first wave raced into the harbour.

Dalton shook his head in sympathy as he looked at the harbour and William in one of the lifeboats with the *Meigle*'s crew, a sack of flour on each slim shoulder. He guessed, rightly, that the young man was pleased to have something useful to do after a week of loss.

"It's three houses gone, Captain, sir," William called up. "Three houses."

"My God," Dalton responded. "And how many dead?"

"Well, sir, we've done nothing but bury people here in Point au Gaul lately," came the sombre reply. The *Meigle* crew members laid down their sacks of flour and balanced themselves in the lifeboat to listen.

"Miss Mary Ann Walsh and Mrs. Eliza Walsh, they lived together in a house that was over there," William said, pointing. "They were washed away. We got their bodies, first one and then the other. And it was the funniest thing—we found a tin box full of money, completely dry mind you, next to Miss Mary Ann's body. When the women laid it out for counting, it covered a double bed. They gave it to Miss Mary Ann's church, as she would have wanted."

"Who else died, son?" Dalton asked, his cheeks pink at the young man's familiarity.

"Well, poor Thomas Hillier was killed, unaccountably so, really," William answered.

"How's that?" one of the crew asked shyly, letting his curiosity get the better of him.

"Well, for one thing, he wasn't supposed to be home," William explained. "He worked all over the country as a fish oil inspector and he only came home to celebrate his birthday, first time he ever did. It's a funny thing, an odd thing."

"The whole tidal wave is strange," Dalton said.

"It is, sir," William answered. "And very sad. But the saddest part of it is those that's left behind. Lydia Hillier, Thomas' widow, is expecting a baby any day now and she had two other young children, Caroline and little Benjamin, and she has no one to support her."

Dalton's face blanched at the thought. He looked at the clear sea water and his eye took in bread dough in pans sitting on the harbour bottom, as if that's where they belonged.

William continued. "She was Thomas' second wife and she lives with his two grown children, Harold and Georgina. Now I don't know what's to become of her. That was their family home, the Hilliers'—I suppose the older children can claim the house, Thomas' grown children. They might—they aren't too fond of Lydia, never took to her."

Dalton silently thought of how complicated village life always was, though artists and poets might render it simple and romantic. His own visits to his father's hometown on the Southern Shore had taught him this. Meanwhile, he wondered how many Lydias he would come across on this sad voyage.

169

"That's three deaths so far, young man," he said gently, trying to prod William on.

"Well, the worst of it is the Hilliers, not the same Hilliers as Thomas, a different family altogether," Lockyer said. "Mrs. Lizzie Hillier had her four grandchildren with her. Irene was over for a quick visit, her mother, Jemima, said. But her daughter, Jessie Hipditch's three were there for the night. Their house was just about there, right near the water."

As William pointed and paused, Dalton and the men stared at the emptiness that now took the place of Lizzie Hillier's house.

"And now they're all gone," William said simply. "David and Jessie Hipditch lost their three children. Poor Jessie is out of her mind with all of them gone. Her sister, Jemima, is not far behind her with the loss of her only daughter, Irene."

"Who has lost their homes?" Dalton asked after a minute.

"David and Jessie, sir," William answered. "On top of losing their children, they lost their home, too, though Jessie doesn't even care about that. They're staying with Jessie's sister, Nan. And Henry Hillier, he's Mrs. Lizzie's husband—his house is gone. He's staying with Nan, too. He doesn't want to rebuild. He thinks he's too old. He's sixty-nine. He says his wife is dead and four of his grandchildren are dead. My father thinks he's lost the will to live. And if you lose that, my father says, you're finished."

"Your father's right, son," Dalton said, stroking his chin, slowly, still surveying what remained of the Point au Gaul infrastructure. He couldn't imagine how the people could rebuild in time for next year's fishing season, not this close to winter, when they had enough to do to get enough wood to heat, repair, and rebuild their homes. In this part of the country they had to travel so far to get wood. He wondered when the tradition of going to winter quarters had died out here and why.

The people here had so much need of wood now, they would have to buy it. Most people didn't have that kind of extra cash, however. Dalton had been all over the island. If Point au Gaul was like most outports, there'd be a few families with five hundred dollars or a thousand dollars in the bank or salted away in their kitchen somewhere, and another handful with a hundred dollars or two hundred dollars, but the majority would have very little or none at all, maybe twenty dollars here or there. Most of the time there wasn't much call for money. Fish was the currency of their lives, not dollar notes. In any case, that, too, had been swept away by the big sea.

When William Lockyer and members of the *Meigle* crew returned in the lifeboat, Dalton walked across the deck to them.

"Lockyer," he said. "Did you find their bodies?"

"Which bodies, Captain, sir?"

"Oh, the children, I mean, the children," Dalton stammered. "Did you find their bodies?"

"We did, sir," William answered. "We got Jessie's three little ones that night and the women laid them out. But we didn't get poor Irene for awhile. Her being missing was making Jemima's grief all the more unbearable. We only got her body early yesterday morning. Her father, Joshua, found her washed up on the beach over there, just before you came in. He went searching every morning at dawn. He was determined to get her. Poor little thing, all beat up on the rocks like that and waterlogged. But the only thing missing was her left overshoe. She's laid out up there now, though I think they got her covered, poor girl."

Dalton stifled his retching. He said nothing. He tried to think of sharing a pot of tea with Cora in the breakfast room in their St. John's home. He walked back and forth on deck as the men loaded the lifeboats with sugar, flour, and tea.

As they prepared to head into Point au Gaul again, he said, "William, you didn't tell me about the third family made homeless."

"Oh, it's poor old John Walsh, Captain, sir," William said. "He's an old bachelor in ill health these days. All his gear and food is gone, too. He's awfully upset. The women are trying to console him. Don't know what he'll do from now on..."

The young man's voice faded away and Dalton's sea green eyes fixed on a little house that stood with its back to the water. It's a wonder the waves didn't take that as a dare, he thought. He had spent his entire life on the water and had seen men swallowed by spume, crushed by sea ice, and numbed into statues by salt-water crystals. But never had he seen the Atlantic so cruel as the waves that had laced Point au Gaul that November night.

21

At Lamaline, Captain Dalton's brow would finally have a chance to unfurrow a little. There, the members of the area committee sat down in the ship's galley with the expedition personnel, all of whom were following the path taken by Nurse Cherry and the local men who escorted her. The members of the committee representing the strip of land from High Beach to Lord's Cove introduced themselves quietly. They included C.C. Pittman, a Justice of the Peace and the committee's chair, Father Sullivan, and Lewis Crews.

"You know about the tragedies that have visited Point au Gaul," Pittman said slowly. "But no one has died here in Lamaline."

"Thanks be to God," Father Sullivan whispered.

Captain Dalton took a crumpled handkerchief from his jacket pocket and wiped the sweat off his forehead. He blinked rapidly.

"That's not to say there isn't a great deal of devastation," Pittman continued. "Many stages have been damaged or swept away entirely. Dozens of trap skiffs are gone... it's the same all along the coast, of course. And there's even worse..."

"Yes," said Father Sullivan, speaking with a firmer voice now. "Poor Mrs. Hipditch, Fred's wife. She has no house anymore. It's quite beyond repair, I can assure you of that. The family has six children—the two eldest boys have just started fishing with their father but Fred is away in Corner Brook working on the new mill there, I believe. Poor Mrs. Hipditch has lost their store, their Madeira fish, and some food as well. It's a sad case."

The priest lowered his grey head. Captain Dalton studied him.

"Jim Hooper, too," Lewis Crews piped up. "Jim and Lucy, their house is all beaten up and their stage is, too. Jim is not even in good health."

"Perhaps we can talk to some of these people and see what they think about their future," Dr. Campbell suggested, taking a slim pen out of his breast pocket.

"Jim's still over in St. Pierre," Crews responded. "He hasn't been able to get back yet."

Campbell's right eye widened.

"Oh, for goodness' sake," Fudge, the M.H.A., said. "People here go to St. Pierre for all sorts of reasons, not just to get a bottle of rum. Many of them even have family over there. There's a long history of marriages between people here and the French."

"There is no need for your rash reaction," Campbell answered, turning to his government colleague. "I implied nothing sinister at all. I just wondered how Mr. Hooper could travel, given his ill health."

There was a moment of silence before Dalton broke it.

"I'm governed by the weather, gentlemen," he said. "We have to keep a close eye on it, this being late November. So I suggest we keep these meetings to the minimum time possible and do our business in as expedient a manner as possible. Our focus here has to be on assessing the need and getting supplies to the victims. We've got a fair bit of ground to cover yet." Then he added with the slightest of tremors in his voice, "And I'm sure we want to do everything we can for these stricken people."

Before the group dispersed, the South Coast Disaster Committee had commandeered all the stocks of coal available in Lamaline and Minister Lake had dispatched a ship from the town to North Sydney, Nova Scotia, Canada to get more coal for use in the villages of the southern Burin Peninsula. The committee also telegraphed an order of clothes to stores in the town of Fortune. A truck filled with dresses, coats, pants, and boots arrived in Lamaline that same afternoon. When the members of the local committee handed the new clothes out to families from High Beach to Lord's Cove, frozen mouths broke into smiles for the first time since the great waves hit the shores that awful night. Little girls twirled on their toes, letting their new dresses blow full. Boys hitched up their new dungarees and nodded proudly. For the first time in days, the children of Allan's Island and Point au Gaul began to feel like they wanted to put their coats on and go out to play.

But everything Captain Dalton feared about Taylor's Bay turned out to be true. As the *Meigle* approached the harbour—quiet as a graveyard though it was midday—Dalton gripped the ship's rail and drew his breath in. He made a grim count; only five of the original seventeen houses in Taylor's Bay remained standing.

"Very worrying," said Dr. Mosdell. "All those people crowded into those few houses, and they're small houses at that. It's a health menace to be sure. If one gets a serious sickness, it'll spread like wildfire."

Suddenly heads began emerging from windows and from the sides of buildings; they put Dalton in mind of snails coming out of their shells. How different it is from sailing into a port and everyone comes out to the wharf to meet you, he thought. These poor people almost look afraid. Once outside, they went no farther than their windows and doors; they stood there, waiting.

On Mosdell's orders, the medical staff left the ship and dispersed to the five remaining houses, doctor's kits in hand.

When Nurse Rendell from the *Meigle* reached Deborah and Sydney Woodland's house, she entered and said, "I'm so sorry for what's happened..." Then she stopped, looked around at the cluster of people in the Woodlands' kitchen and continued, "But you seem in better shape that I expected."

"Nurse Cherry's been here," came a little voice from a corner of the room. "And she told us what to do!"

Deborah smiled. "She did. And we were lucky. We lost no food and I've been sparing it along. You'll want to tend to some people, though. They're homeless and have no prospects at all for the winter."

Deborah motioned toward a row of children who sat on a sunken daybed. The nurse nodded and turned in their direction. The girls and boys lazily swung their legs back and forth, the biggest child scuffing her bare feet on the floor.

"We'll get shoes for her," Nurse Rendell offered, smiling brightly.

"Their mothers are in the parlour," Deborah said, in a quieter voice. "They say they don't want to stay in Taylor's Bay. They want to go to Fortune where they've got friends and family. They think they'll be safer there."

Suddenly Nurse Rendell felt someone behind her. She turned abruptly and saw a small woman with great black eyes in a face the colour of the moon.

"I'll not stay in this harbour another winter," she said firmly. "I can't stand the thought of it."

Nurse Rendell opened her mouth to speak but closed it again when she saw the firmness in the woman's jaw.

That night three women and their youngest children slept on board the *Meigle*. The mothers had shaken Captain Dalton's hand, pumping it, as they climbed onto the ship. Fudge, the M.H.A., had taken the Taylor's Bay refugees under his wing; he'd see to it that they got clothing and boots once the *Meigle* arrived in Burin, he announced. Then he would travel west to Fortune Bay with them on the *Glencoe*.

Now, in the sharp night air, Captain Dalton stood at the wheel as the little party slept below, feeling safer than they had in well over a week. He laughed softly at the irony of how being on waves rather than land reassured and comforted them. He would tell Cora about this, he thought, and, next to the fire, they would have a grand discussion about the complexities of the human mind.

"She was reluctant to come, Captain," Dr. Mosdell tut-tutted as he made his way onto the *Meigle*, tied up in St. Lawrence harbour after a snowy and windswept morning. "But I did manage to get her here."

"Welcome on board the *Meigle*, Nurse Cherry," Captain Dalton said formally, bowing his fair head to the slightly stooped woman following the doctor up the gangplank. He could see that beneath her cap, her brown hair was unkempt and her eyes were narrow in the manner of one who has recently awakened. He guessed that Mosdell had woken her. Doctors are odd beings, he thought.

"If anyone deserves a rest, it's you, Nurse Cherry," Dalton said firmly.

"I should have thought that if anyone deserves a rest, it would be you, Captain!" Nurse Cherry answered quickly.

Dalton drew back at the sharpness in her voice. He stepped back to let her pass.

"One of the nurses will show you to a cabin, Nurse Cherry," he said. "We hope you'll be most comfortable on board."

Nurse Cherry stood erect and grimaced. She studied the deck and then the captain. "I don't know who gave the orders to bring me on board," she snapped. "But I had work to do, plenty of it, and I was interrupted in my tasks."

"I beg your pardon, Ma'am," Dr. Mosdell said, suppressing a smile. "You were, in fact, prone on a daybed when I found you."

Nurse Cherry's mouth opened wide but no sound emerged.

"I mean, Nurse Cherry," the doctor continued. "Not that you were sleeping the days away or that you had neglected your duty in any way. I mean that you had travelled along the entire shore in the worst kind of weather and in so doing had worked yourself into a state of exhaustion, so much so that you had collapsed in the middle of the day in a stranger's house."

Nurse Cherry's mouth still gaped open.

"Ma'am, Dr. Mosdell is only concerned about your health," Captain Dalton interjected. "As we all are. As we have moved from one village to another, we have heard about your visits, made on horseback and on foot, and your work, done at all hours of the night and day. Do you not think it is time for a rest?"

"I am only tired, that's all, not grief-stricken, like my patients. If I rest, what shall happen to these people?" Nurse Cherry said, her face the colour of a ripening tomato. "After all they have been through."

"You are not alone now," Dr. Mosdell answered. "We have a medical staff on board, physicians and nurses both. The people here are no longer entirely dependent on you. The burden is off you alone."

Dalton waited for a look of relief to cross Nurse Cherry's face but it did not come. Instead, her mouth remained hard and her chin, held defiantly high.

"Gentlemen," she said finally. "I resent the way you took me out of that home, making the decision yourself and taking charge of me as if I am not in my right mind."

Mosdell and Dalton exchanged quick glances.

"My responsibility as a doctor extends to you, too, Nurse Cherry," Mosdell said quietly. "When I see a woman exerted beyond a point that is safe, I have to do something about it, as you know. I think now we ought not to spend more time discussing it. It is cold up here, don't you think? Shall we have some tea down below?"

"I don't think I want any tea right now," Nurse Cherry answered.

"Come with me, Nurse Cherry," Captain Dalton said. "I'll find Nurse Rendell. She'll show you what a comfortable bunk we've prepared for you."

He breathed a low sigh when the Englishwoman followed him to the cabin. In the hallway he introduced her to Nurse Rendell and turned quickly on his heel when he had passed her over. Up top again, he met Mosdell.

"We'll have her in Burin tomorrow," he told the doctor. "And she can rest there a couple of days. I've arranged return passage for her on the *Argyle*."

"Well!" laughed Dr. Mosdell. "She could certainly use the rest! She's wound up as tight as a drum!"

Dalton thought of Cora and the kind words she unfailingly had for her elderly and frequently contrary aunts.

"She's been through a lot," he said ploddingly. "She's tired and overwrought, poor woman."

Before the *Meigle* pulled out of St. Lawrence, the expedition party met with the local committee and charged them with supervising relief measures as they had with their counterparts elsewhere. Meanwhile, Captain Dalton and his crew took account of the damage the *tsunami* had done to the town. The harbour was desolate; all the stores and stages on both its sides had been swept away. Little black lumps of coal floated in the harbour, like a torment to the cold people on shore. The winds blew dark ash off them. Cracked oars drifted in on the beach. Thwarts, broken in two, flopped onto the rocks, in a blunt offering. Women could only glance hard at these things and close their eyes. The men tried hard not to think of spring when the fish would start coming in. How would they catch it?

When news of the situation at St. Lawrence reached Magistrate Hollett in Burin, he telegraphed Prime Minister

Squires in the capital. As Squires read of the devastation in St. Lawrence, the largest settlement in the area, he clutched his chin tight and sucked in his breath. His face grew white as he realized that every time a message came from the South Coast the picture was more grave than originally thought. Worries over the disaster invaded his every thought. Squires lay awake night after night, shifting helplessly in his bed, wondering if his government had sent enough supplies. How would his government pay for the rest? It was almost a month now since the stock market crashed and the meaning of that event was beginning to sink in. As the days went by, the administration in St. John's still did not have a good fix on the death toll on the lower portion of the stricken peninsula. That would only come with a full report from the *Meigle*.

Still the dire messages from Burin kept coming. When Hollett visited St. Lawrence, soon after the *Meigle* left, he wrote to Squires: "The people are in a state of dire destitution. Immediate assistance is necessary."

There was, though, no loss of life at St. Lawrence. The people had seen the waves coming and had headed for higher ground. Though rebuilding their town would be a long, hard task, men and women would sometimes cast their eyes to the sky and bless themselves, murmuring prayers of gratitude that no one had died that terrible night.

22

In Burin, Captain Dalton saw that Nurse Cherry had an escort to take her to the home of the local Nonia nurse, where she could stay and rest for a couple of days before returning home to Lamaline. She smiled as she left the ship, to his relief.

"Thank you for kidnapping me, Captain," she said.

Dalton smiled back, almost confident that she was joking.

The skipper's first order of business here was to meet with Magistrate Hollett so the two men could bring each other up-to-date on the aftermath of the *tsunami*. When everything was straightened away on the *Meigle*, Dalton walked to Hollett's home with the magistrate who had come to the dock to greet him. The captain noted that Hollett hadn't lost any of the worried look he wore when Dalton first met him the other day.

"My wife has hardly seen me in days," Hollett said. "And Lucy is so patient."

*

The two men sat in Hollett's dark parlour on overstuffed chairs sipping tea that needed warming. In the high-ceilinged quiet of the place, Dalton could almost forget the high dose of tragedy he'd wit nessed in recent hours. But Hollett leaned forward, eagerly.

"One of the strange things," he said, "is that men from the schooners reported no disturbance at sea. The first inkling they had of disaster came from the debris they saw floating past. And what a sight that was...very unexpected, indeed, as you would know more than me, Captain."

"That's the way these *tsunamis* work, sir," Dalton responded. "It's the land that gets the damage, not the sea. They're not storms at sea, at all. If you're close to shore, you'll feel a swell, but that's all. I've never experienced one, myself, and I wasn't out that night. I was safe at home in St. John's where we thought there was an explosion at the mines on Bell Island, due to the noise the great wave made. Later I heard that St. John's harbour had emp-tied for a few minutes. Then I knew there'd been a *tsunami*, or tidal wave, most people call it. But I knew old fellows who've seen the devastation they cause in the Indian Ocean and places south. They wreck entire villages and towns—people sometimes move away rather than rebuild in some cases. Never heard them do much damage this far north, though."

"Nor have I," Hollett answered. Dalton noted that he was wide-eyed in the manner of someone who still didn't believe what was happening.

"We ran out of drugs on board," Dalton reported. "There were a lot of sick people. Mosdell and the others, the nurses, said there was a lot of call for drugs because so many people don't have enough bedclothes and they're living in overcrowded conditions, passing on illnesses to each other. Then the shock and grief made them more vulnerable to illness."

"So what did you do?"

"We went to St. Pierre and got more supplies. We were in Lamaline, which isn't far from the French islands, when we ran out. And we knew there were just no stocks left anywhere on the Burin Peninsula. I must say, the French medical people were so helpful. The French authorities, too—they readily offered their port facilities to us most generously."

"And thank God St. Pierre and Miquelon weren't affected by the tidal wave," Hollett added. "So far from their own government in Paris."

"We didn't bring sufficient building supplies, either," Dalton said. "So I ordered ten thousand feet of lumber through the Manager of the Railway to go there on the *Argyle*. On the *Meigle* we had roofing supplies, nails, and glass, and we gave all that away, though, as I say, it was not nearly enough for every community."

As Hollett spoke of the wreckage in the immediate area, Dalton sank into the overstuffed leather chair. He fixed his eyes on the intensity on the magistrate's face. These were Hollett's people, he realized—his family, friends, and neighbours.

The *Meigle* departed Burin on November 27 and dispatched the members of the relief expedition at Argentia at nine o'clock in the morning, where they caught the train. They were in St. John's a few hours later, rushing to the prime minister's office.

Squires was almost silent as he listened to Mosdell's account of the destruction the tidal wave had wrought.

"The property losses are heaviest at St. Lawrence," the doctor said.

The prime minister nodded.

"It's to be expected, I suppose," Mosdell continued. "It being the largest town on the boot."

"Hollett keeps writing me," Squires said slowly. "About the loss of life in particular. It's greater than first thought, I've learned."

"Twenty-seven," Campbell said. "That's the most accurate figure. Almost all women and children."

Squires walked slowly around his large desk. The only sound in the room was his assistant's breathing.

From behind his desk, the prime minister seemed to return to himself.

"There may be a solution at hand—to the damage, I mean," he announced. "A South Coast Disaster Committee, under the governor's patronage, was formed at a public meeting two nights ago. I'm the honorary president and Horwood is acting as chair. Hollett suggested a public subscription. A good idea. But the people were ahead of him—as I knew they would be." He smiled; his colleagues smiled back in recognition of Squires' trademark expression.

"They've begun house to house collections all over the city," he continued. "And benefit concerts are being arranged."

Mosdell nodded.

"The *Evening Telegram* has opened a public subscription as well," he added. "That family has got to get in on everything. Hmmph! Well, they've got ten thousand dollars together for us in just a few days. According to what Hollett says and

what you tell me, we'll need every cent. All these public donations take pressure off the government. We'll need the help
after the true impact of the New York stock market crash
begins to be felt."

The other men said nothing for a few minutes. Then Campbell
spoke up. "I'm sure other towns in the country will open their
hearts and pocketbooks as well," he said.

"Oh indeed!" Squires responded enthusiastically. "They've
set up a subcommittee on outport contact. I've been told to
expect large contributions from Grand Falls and Corner Brook in
particular, where the paper mills are located."

As Minister of Marine and Fisheries, Lake's thoughts drifted
to the hundreds of fishing villages on the northeast and west
coast. He knew they were filled with people who would want to
help but, like their counterparts on the south coast, cash was not
important in their lives—fish was their currency.

"Is there a way for people to give non-cash gifts?" he asked.

"Oh yes," Squires said. "A Kinds Committee has been set up
to receive food and clothing and these have begun pouring in
already. Harveys Ltd. has donated warehouse space near the railway station where everything can be stored before it's sent to the
Burin Peninsula."

Lake's mind harkened back to the snow and wind that had
slowed the *Meigle*'s voyage along the coast.

"What are the plans for getting donations to the South
Coast?" he asked. "And distributing them?"

"Hollett has stepped up to the plate," Squires answered con-
fidently. "We've appointed him the committee's agent. He'll settle
the claims in a just and expedient manner."

"It'll be a massive job," Lake said gravely. "He'll need every support." The other members of the relief expedition nodded and murmured "yes."

"It's a great relief that almost no breadwinners were killed," Squires said, looking out the window now.

"It is, sir," Mosdell said. "But it is an extremely serious situation all the same because hundreds of fishermen are in no position to earn a living this coming fishing season."

"Literally thousands of fishing outbuildings are destroyed, completely flattened," Lake added. "It is no easy task to rebuild them, especially in winter and without easy access to lumber."

"Quite a few of them are grief-stricken, too," Campbell said. "Having lost relatives, wives even, to the tidal wave."

Squires turned away from the window and nodded. For a moment, a white cast returned to his face. Then he said, "That may be so. But our people are tough and resourceful, especially those in the outports. And the committee will give them the means to rebuild. I have great faith that everything is in hand."

He glanced around the ornate room.

"I thank you all, gentlemen, for the service you have rendered to our country as members of the relief expedition."

Mosdell had been about to ask Squires about further assistance from the Newfoundland government, but the prime minister had already disappeared from his office and was dashing down the hallway.

23

Some of the tension in Magistrate Hollett's shoulders was finally released when he received news that the South Coast Disaster Committee had been formed and had begun receiving public donations from all over the country. His heart leapt when he heard that money had begun to trickle in from the United States, Canada, and England as well. It was all badly needed, he knew, and he would make sure it would be put to good use.

One of the villages Hollett was most concerned about was Port au Bras, another peninsula community with French roots. Migratory fishermen from St. Malo, France, christened the village "port of arms," which might have been an indication of the sporadic ethnic conflicts over cod that marked Newfoundland history. By the late 1700s, both English and French settlers had made Port au Bras their permanent home, living in a collection of houses that seemed to tumble onto the rocks and almost into the sea. By 1900, three hundred people lived in the village. Known for its

skilled fishing captains and masters of foreign-going trading vessels, there was something of the invincible about Port au Bras.

That ended on the night of November 18, as Port au Bras
native Ern Cheeseman wrote in a letter to his brother, Jack:

> *Monday evening at 5.20 we had an earth tremor, all
> the houses and the ground shook for about 5 minutes.
> This put everyone in a panic. Women screamed and
> prayed and we stood silent and scared but we were just
> trying and had finally succeeded in quieting the women
> when we had a tidal wave of the worst kind. Enormous
> waves twenty feet high swept into the harbour...*
>
> *Charlie Clarke's store went first, taking Henry
> Dibbon's with it into the Pond, taking everything as it
> came with a thunderous roar. It swept around by
> Ambrose's up to Jack Bennett's out our way bringing all
> the stores and houses that stood in its way. Then all the
> boats went mad (and) came in.*
>
> *The harbour was cleaned (by) the first wave. Then
> the second one came and brought it all in again. Such
> noise and scrunching you never heard.*
>
> *By this time we had all fled to the hills, the highest
> places we could find. From there we watched the third
> wave come and go. You could hear the poor humans who
> were caught, screaming women and men praying out
> loud. Oh God, Jack, it was terrible...*

Fifty-three-year-old Tom Fudge had been in his stores with his two
sons, John and Job, when the ground began to tremble. John, just
entering his twenties, laughed at the unexpected sensation. Job, at
thirteen, blanched and looked to his father for words of comfort.

"You're not scared, are you, Job?" John teased.

Before Tom could answer, his wife, Jessie, appeared at the
door, followed by the couple's three daughters, Gertie, fifteen,

Harriet, eleven, and Hannah, only nine. The two youngest girls held hands and Tom noticed that Hannah was walking on her tip-toes as if to protect herself from the rumbling of the earth.

"What's going on, Tom?" Jessie asked urgently.

"I don't really know," her husband answered. "It must be some kind of earthquake, though they're not generally known in Newfoundland. Usually they happen in warmer parts."

"God save us!" said Jessie.

He looked at his daughters and then at white-faced Job.

"It won't last long," he said. "And it won't be a powerful one like they have in the West Indies. Don't fret now."

Little Hannah looked up from under her chestnut curls and smiled at him. Tom winked at her. As the tremor died away, Jessie shooed her girls back to the house. Tom watched their long skirts swish as his wife and daughters went inside.

Not long afterwards, a wall of seawater rushed into the Fudges' garden and pulled the family's house away with it. Tom was still working in the nearby store with his sons. Oddly, the smell of kelp and salt filled Tom's nostrils before he heard the roar of the wave. The smell jolted him and he jumped to the doorway to see rushing grey water where his house had been. He let out a deep cry and froze. Then he shouted at John and Job, "Get to high ground! Move! Quick!"

The boys ran from the store toward the hills, joining their panicked neighbours. At one point John turned around and called, "Come on, Dad!"

But he could no longer see his father.

From the high land, Ern Cheeseman and dozens of other people saw Tom Fudge's store swallowed by the tail end of the wave.

They could hear the screams of women and children trapped in houses borne on the tidal wave, Jessie Fudge and her three daughters, among them. In short order, the first wave had torn eleven houses from the ground. It drove Bill and Mary Clarke's two-storey, eight room house into Path End, a neighbouring inlet, where it would have to be towed down. It destroyed the house of Gus and Jessie Abbott and their six children and that of their kin, John and Annie Abbott, and their seven children. It swept away the house of eighty-one-year-old pensioner William Allen. Tom Fudge's brother Job, after whom his younger son had been named, was in poor health; now his house was gone. John Dibbon, who lived alone, was homeless. So was sixty-seven-year-old Mary Dibbon, who was widowed by the *tsunami*. The house Thomas Brenton was building for his new wife, Alice, was engulfed by the tidal wave. Four of the Cheeseman households lost their homes to the violent water that night: those of fifty-five-year-old widower Thomas; twenty-three-year-old bachelor Joseph; and married couple, Jeremiah and Harriet, both fifty-seven.

As the first wave emptied the harbour, Ern Cheeseman and the others tried to follow what was happening, though their eyes could scarcely comprehend it. They tried to count the houses that were hauled up, and then to figure out who was on the high ground and who wasn't. Ern saw young Job Fudge shivering on the hill not far away. Though he was well-dressed for a November evening, Ern realized the boy must be in shock. He approached young Job.

"Where's the rest of your family, Job?" he asked gently.

"John is near the bottom of the hill trying to find Dad," Job answered, his eyes staring at the dot below that represented his brother.

"And where did you last see your father?" Ern persisted quietly.

"Our house is gone and Dad's gone to get it," Job said. "Mommy and Gertie and Harriet and Hannah are in it. Dad's gone to rescue them."

"Take my jacket, Job," Ern said, laying his coat over the boy's shoulders. "It's getting a little chilly."

Ern leaned back on a boulder that emerged from the earth and buried his face in his hands. There wasn't a single store left in the harbour. The houses were all out to sea now. He couldn't see Tom Fudge from where he sat. He could hardly see Job's older brother. His helplessness was in danger of congealing into red hot anger unless he did something with it.

He rose again.

"Job, you stay right here," he said. "Don't move. Promise me that. I'm going to get your brother."

Ern bolted down the hill until he reached John.

"Come up to the high ground with me," he ordered the young man. "Your little brother needs you."

"I've got to find Dad," John protested. "Mother and the girls are swept away."

"I know," Ern said. "I'm sorry. But that wave is going to come in again—look at how empty the harbour is. And it might take you with it if you stay here. At this point you seem to be all Job has."

John froze. "But my Dad... I... I..."

"Come with me," Ern said, quietly but firmly.

John looked at the sea, then turned to follow his neighbour.

"We've got to hurry," Ern added.

On top of the hill, Job's shivering seemed to have subsided a little. The boy collapsed into his brother's arms when he saw John. Not long after John and Ern reached the high ground, the second wave bombed its way into Port au Bras. It was even louder than the first. Now the hill was filled with the sound of mournful praying and cries of anguish and grief. The sobs of the Fudge brothers came full force now. They knew they had lost their sisters and their parents and were all alone in the world. Ern Cheeseman and their uncles and aunts made a ring around them in a vain effort to shield them from the pain they would feel for a lifetime.

The people of Port au Bras barely noticed the third wave, which tossed clapboard, barrels, and the remains of battered boats about the harbour. Turnips, heads of cabbage, and pieces of salt meat floated on the water. Ern Cheeseman wrote:

> *Everybody is miserable, nervous wrecks and in need of help immediately. All people who had food for the winter lost it in their stores. We must have flour, sugar, tea, molasses, beef, and pork immediately... Everything we have is gone and we are ruined...everything is dismal and breaks one's heart to look at the harbour and then think of what it was like fifteen minutes before this terrible calamity.*

Most worrying was the loss of boats and the damage to those that survived the *tsunami*. A schooner was damaged to the tune of one thousand dollars and its two large banking dories—which four fishermen worked from—swept away. A twenty-two-ton western boat needed repairs that would also cost a thousand dollars.

Eighteen-year-old Francis Bennett was in severe shock, long after the villagers emerged from the hill. His fifty-eight-year-old mother, Mary Ann, died in the tidal wave, as did his fifty-year-old uncle, Henry Dibbon. The young entrepreneur's business was also completely destroyed. Francis believed in getting an early start in life; still a teenager, he was already married and a successful trader. Gone were his flakes, stages, trap skiff, banking dory, a thousand feet of lumber, a staysail, 145 yards of ducksail, ten oil casks, Fairbanks weights, and weighing beams and weights—losses worth $1,500.00. Though a young man, Francis was overwhelmed at the thought of starting all over again from nothing, especially in the face of his grief.

Yet, like many around Burin, Port au Bras was a prosperous village. John Bennett, who owned the damaged western boat, had $280 in the bank. John Dibbon, who was also without shelter and whose brother Henry had died, had two thousand dollars in the bank. George and Elizabeth Bennett, whose house had shifted four feet, breaking their two chimneys, had thirty-five dollars cash on them as well as $1,500 in a savings account. Not everyone was well off, though; fifty-four-year-old Ellen Brenton cried over the twenty gallons of berries she'd picked and the sea had stolen from her.

The waves weren't long gone when they began to find the bodies. In Ern Cheeseman's words, "No human had a chance in such raging roaring seas." Within two days, the body of eighty-four-year-old Louisa Allen, a native of Oderin, was found tucked under one of the remaining houses. A fisherman in Path End, two miles away, came across the bodies of Jessie Fudge and two of her daughters, Harriet May and little Hannah. That of fifteen-year-old Gertie was still missing. Mary Ann Bennett's body was discovered under what was left of the government wharf.

As darkness grew thick on the night of November 18, the people of Port au Bras gradually became sure that there would be no more waves. Finally, with midnight close at hand, they crept down the hill and back to the houses that were still left. Their shoulders were slumped and they walked hesitantly, their eyes not leaving the moonlit sea.

The brothers, John and Job Fudge, moved slowly with their arms around each other. As they reached the bottom of the hill, near where their family store and house had so recently stood, they saw a hunched figure sitting on the ground. As they got closer, they heard a low moan. Although they had never heard it before, something in the sound sparked a deep recognition and they strode toward the figure.

"My God, it's Dad!" John cried, stooping down to look into his father's haggard face.

"Dad!" Job cried, falling to his knees and hugging his father.

Tom burst into tears and let out loud sobs.

"I saw them in the window!" he cried. "I couldn't get to them..."

The boys began crying again.

"They just went by on that wave," Tom continued, gulping air between sobs. "I followed the house. But I couldn't do anything."

"Oh Daddy," Job cried. He crawled into his father's lap, picturing his mother and sisters desperate for rescue as they were swept out to sea. He knew he would never see them again.

Tom's brother and his wife, Mary, had caught up to the little group.

"Thank God you're alive!" Mary said. "We thought you were gone, too."

"It's a miracle you weren't," her husband said. "Staying on the low ground like that."

Mary elbowed him in the ribs. "He had to try to get Jessie and the girls," she said.

Tom began to moan again, but this time he pulled his sons close to him. Their relatives and neighbours stood around them in the cool November night.

"Come home with us, Tom," Sam Green said.

"Or with us, Tom," Bridget Hardstone said.

"You're welcome at our place, too, Tom," Sarah Hynes said. "For as long as you like."

24

Magistrate Malcolm Hollett was determined to fully document every single case from Mortier Bay in the north to the villages of the boot around to Fortune Bay on the other side of the peninsula. The town of Fortune had survived the *tsunami* virtually untouched, but forty-three-year-old widower Edgar Hillier had seen his house ripped off its foundation and thrown onto a high rock; in addition, the home's porch and an annex had been destroyed. Hillier was in poor health, was going blind, and had three children who depended on him.

On the other side of the peninsula in Mortier near Marystown, the waves washed John and Bridget Antle's house off its foundation. It would have to be taken down and rebuilt... Hollett nearly cracked his pen as he spread the words across the page. Then he glanced at a map; Mortier was just the beginning.

In mid-December Hollett called a meeting of the Rock Harbour-Corbin Committee. He had made several trips down the coast and was fair bursting to talk of what he had seen. Although he was now the agent for the South Coast Disaster Committee, the magistrate wanted to show his closest neighbours that he had not forgotten them.

As snowdrifts piled up outside Hollett's Burin house, three men walked up the path. Merchant Frank LeFeuvre came from Bull's Cove. He was followed by Albert Grant of Corbin and Captain William Foote who came from Stepaside.

As the men settled into the parlour and were served tea by Hollett's quiet little maid, the magistrate read his draft report on the district south of Burin.

The men nodded solemnly and Albert Grant spoke up.

"Make sure you mention that Joshua Mayo's house is gone," he offered. "His and Sophia's. The first wave ripped the house off its foundation and broke away the porch. It tore great holes in the roof, too. Now there's a big tribe of them homeless."

Hollett picked up his pen and raised his bushy eyebrows.

"There's the Mayo children," Grant continued. "Morgan, Irene, and Daisy, and there's the four Moulton orphans who live with them, Annie and Tryphena, and the boys, little William and Bert. They lost all their food and Josh's Hubbard engine is badly damaged, too."

"Sounds like a very sad case," Hollett said grimly.

"It is," Grant nodded. "Those orphans have been through enough already and now this. I believe the family is all split up because there are too many of them to be housed together. It must be hard on those poor children."

After a minute, Hollett turned his attention to merchant Frank LeFeuvre.

"How did you make out in the tidal wave, Frank? Have you had a chance to assess everything yet?" he asked.

"Well, it was the business that was hurt," LeFeuvre answered. "Not our home, thanks be to God. But LeFeuvre's Trading Company took a hit—I'd put the damage at about twenty-one hundred dollars. It's substantial for us."

Hollett looked dour. "You'll need to be back in business for the fishing season," he said. "The fishermen will need that as much as you do. This brings me to my next topic. There's been a generous response to our tragedy from all over the country and beyond. We very much need and appreciate all the help we can get. But now Christmas is coming and the New Year will follow. People's attention will turn from the tidal wave. Besides, human nature being what it is, November 18 will fade from memory soon enough—as good as people are. We have to do something about this."

He stopped and did a slow turn about the parlour as the men considered his words.

"We still need help," Albert Grant said. "There's so much to be done yet."

Hollett continued. "Yes. So I propose a trip to St. John's after Christmas to remind the government and the people of the city of our tragedy and the conditions we are still facing. I think that you three gentlemen should accompany me."

Grant drew back, his eyes wide. LeFeuvre spoke up, "A capital idea, so to speak. A kind of speaking tour of the city."

"It's certainly needed," said Captain Foote. "I don't know if we're the right men to go, but you're on the right track."

"You might want to bring representatives from farther south, where there's even worse damage and grief," Grant said.

Hollett's face brightened. "Quite right!" he said. "Thank you for your support, gentlemen. We shall agree in principle to the idea and begin planning, then?"

He smiled at their nods.

On January 15, 1930 Magistrate Malcolm Hollett and fisherman Albert Grant sat in the editorial offices of *The Daily News* on Duckworth Street in St. John's. Hollett's heavy-lidded eyes bored into the editors and stenographers as he listed off the devastation that the tidal wave had wrought: thirty-two houses destroyed; twenty-seven others badly damaged; 144 large dories and one hundred small dories wrecked; and twenty-seven trap boats smashed to pieces. The men around the table gasped as Hollett spoke. This was the first time they had heard the numbers in such blunt form.

"Our people have also lost much of their fishing gear," Hollett said, speaking slowly. "Gone are forty-seven thousand cotton lines, a hundred and eight herring nets, ninety-four cod nets, thirty caplin seines, and three hundred and fifty six anchors."

"That *is* a great deal of gear," a burly, grey-haired man mused.

"It represents the livelihood of many men like Mr. Grant here," Hollett said. "And some of the wealth of the country, as you can appreciate."

"Rope," Grant said. "We lost over forty thousand fathoms of rope of all sizes."

"Yes," said Hollett. "Keep in mind, gentlemen, that while we are most grateful for everything that has been done for us, the government is only taking care of public property. That is, government wharves will be rebuilt at public expense but family flakes and wharves will not. Our immediate requirements are for timber and sticks for wharves, flakes, and stages. We've received three carloads from Highland, on the west coast of the island, landed by steamer, and we were so pleased to get it. But, sadly, we need more. I've prepared a list of our needs."

He handed a crisp piece of paper to eager hands. It read:

190,000 sticks for flakes
20,000 flake beams
10,000 wharf beams
13,000 flake longers
54,000 two inch planks

"We would be so grateful if your newspaper could publish this list," he added. "It is difficult to distribute the goods we are receiving because so many places are without a wharf or landing stage— Lamaline, Point au Gaul, Taylor's Bay. There's only one private wharf at St. Lawrence. But efforts must be made regardless."

Hollett noted the silence of the editors and how they stared at him. He continued.

"I cannot emphasize how important it is to get the fishermen outfitted for spring. The people of the South Coast are fishermen firstly and lastly and they need to be put in the same position they were in before the disaster."

Albert Grant nodded. "Yes, we are fishermen. We want to fish."

That day, the men of Taylor's Bay put the finishing touches on Charles and Selina Hillier's house, which had sustained fifty dollars worth of damage in the tidal wave, leaving it open on one side and exposed to the winter elements. Through the South Coast Disaster

Committee, fifty thousand feet of lumber had been accumulated. A substantial portion of this had been brought to Taylor's Bay, a priority as per the instructions of the medical staff who had visited on the *Meigle*.

After one of Charles's neighbours hammered in the last nail, he said, "That's it! She's done and ready for you to move back into."

Charles smiled and rubbed his hands in the January cold. He still had a lot of work to do—he had lost his three small boats, stage, and wharf—but this was a start. He looked across the meadow to see Selina and their children, Thomas, Bertram, Junior, Harold, and Freeman, the baby in her arms—his five fine boys. Before the tidal wave, Selina used to talk about wanting a girl; everyday she would tease him about it. Since November 18, she hadn't mentioned the idea.

Behind her was Robert Bonnell, still ashen-faced from the loss of his wife and child to the waves. His three children came after him. The Bonnells would stay with Charles and Selina until the men of the village could build them a new house.

When the group reached the Hillier house, Selina turned to Robert and said, "This is your home now for as long as you like." Charles put his arm around his friend's shoulder. Robert nodded and crossed the threshold, his little ones trailing after him.

Charles and Selina looked at each other. "Poor Robert. I'm so glad we have each other," she said, giving her husband's hand a squeeze. Then she looked into his eyes and smiled shyly.

"Maybe we'll have that girl one day," she said.

That night in Point au Gaul, David Hipditch lay straight as a board in bed, staring at the plastered ceiling as he usually did until sleep finally overtook him in the wee hours just before dawn. The house— not his own, which was at the bottom of the sea somewhere—was full of people, but there seemed to be some kind of cotton gauze between him and everyone else. All his energy went into keeping it well hidden and showing appreciation for the kindness his in-laws, Nan and her family, were showering on him and Jessie. The faces of his and Jessie's drowned children never left him: Thomas' grin; Henry's dancing eyes; little Elizabeth's chubby cheeks. He cursed himself for the thousandth time for not being there to save them from the cruel water. He wished he could talk to Jessie but, though she lay at his side every night, her grief bathed her and there was no room for him in it. Since that awful night, she had barely registered his presence. As he did every night, David tried to pray.

Then he suddenly felt something warm at his shoulder—it was Jessie's face rubbing against him. He turned and looked into her face. She was staring at him, her great brown eyes meeting his. He reached for her long hair and stroked it slowly. She continued to look at him.

"Jessie," he whispered slowly. "I miss them."

Then he cried quietly and she wrapped her arms around him and held him.

"Tell me you love me, Jessie," he pleaded.

"Oh, David," Jessie said. "I love you. I miss my babies, but I love you."

"I need you," David said.

"I'm sorry," his wife answered. "I need you, too."

David pulled Jessie close and they fell into a deep sleep in each other's arms.

AFTERWORD

The 1929 quake originated about 250 kilometres or 153 miles south of the Burin Peninsula and travelled from the epicentre at the astonishing speed of eighty miles per hour. The waves hit the Burin Peninsula villages at sixty-five miles per hour. Although the most damaging by far, it turned out not to have been the first *tsunami* in this part of the world. The first recorded earthquake occurred at Bonavista in 1775. On January 11, 1809, the entire Labrador coast was shaken by earth tremors. On November 30, 1836, people felt the earth rumble in Hopedale, Northern Labrador; at the same time, the air temperature rose considerably. Eight years later, the earth shook at Bonavista again, followed by fierce waves that rushed way inshore. Other earthquakes took place in 1857 in Northern Labrador, this time at Hebron, and in 1890 in St. John's.

Except for reconstructed conversations, this book relies entirely on the historical record and on contributions from witnesses to the *tsunami*, some of whom corresponded with or were interviewed by Flanker Press or the author.

From Part One, young Anna Tarrant of Lawn never forgot the events of November 18, 1929, especially as it was her father's birthday. Recognizing the danger for what it was, Anna's father was responsible for getting many people in his community to safety. Anna grew up to marry an American and became Anna Contois. She wrote to us from her home in Barefoot Bay, Florida.

Mary Kehoe, of Red Head Cove, Conception Bay, who had been sailing to New York with her father, survived the voyage and later married an American. She wrote to us as Mary Dasting from Cape Coral, Florida.

Sam Adams, of Great Burin, who was eleven at the time of the tidal wave and felt the earth move in his garden, wrote to us from London, Ontario.

Bessie Hennebury, of Lord's Cove, almost fifteen, was in her father's fishing room helping to weigh dried fish, when the ground beneath her started to shake, scaring her out the door and up the hill to her home and the illusion of safety. Bessie married Bertram, the son of James Walsh, one of the rescuers of Margaret Rennie, the toddler who was trapped in the floating house with the bodies of her mother, brothers, and sister. Bessie spent her whole life in Lord's Cove.

George and Ernest Pike were the enterprising young brothers of Burin Bay Arm determined to catch Mrs. Moulton's sheep for twenty-five cents—in spite of the earth quaking beneath them. George is still living in Burin Bay Arm, while Ernest left home early during World War II and continued to sail in the foreign trade until he was transferred to the *Abegweit* in the Prince Edward Island-New Brunswick ferry service. He retired as Captain Ernest Pike and wrote to us from Summerside, PEI.

Austin Murphy, of Jersey Room, Lawn, was a seven-year-old boy when the waves gutted the villages of the Burin Peninsula in November, 1929. He had been taking a break from a soccer game when the ground first shook. A retired marine engineer, he wrote to us from Toronto.

Margaret Rennie, of Lord's Cove, the toddler whose survival was considered miraculous when her mother and siblings died in their swept-away house, stayed with her aunt, Minnie Jackman, in Roundabout near St. Lawrence for awhile. Minnie was her late mother, Sarah's, sister. Margaret's brothers, Martin and Albert, stayed with friends. When Margaret was about five she was reunited with her brothers and her father, Patrick, and the family moved to Little St. Lawrence. Patrick went to work in the new fluorspar mines in nearby St. Lawrence and married a local woman. As an adult, Margaret became Margaret Saint and lived in Fox Cove, farther up the Burin Peninsula. There were no photographs of her mother, so she never knew what Sarah looked like.

Part Two recalls the myriad tragedies that befell Taylor's Bay that singular night. There were almost a hundred livyers in the village in 1929. Although the majority of the houses were demolished by the tidal wave, the community seems to have recovered within a few years; by 1935, it had a population of 104, including two new families, the Pikes and the Chafes. After World War II, however, the village went into decline when people began to move away in search of year-round employment.

When I visited Taylor's Bay on a bright fall day in 2003, the only sounds were made by black-backed gulls in search of food on the shore. Most of the few homes near the beach seemed desert ed. The 2003/4 phone book lists only three families for Taylor's Bay. But standing among the grasses that encircle the harbour it is not hard to imagine the boats, wharves, fishing rooms, clapboard homes, and people that once made this achingly beautiful place a community.

Also from Part Two, Nurse Cherry stayed in Lamaline until 1932, thus serving two full contracts with Nonia. Nonia's 1932 Eighth Annual Report delivered at the organization's headquarters in St. John's read:

> *Nurse Cherry remains, as she has been from the first, our 'high liner' in number of patients treated and visits paid. She has given 624 treatments in the Dispensary and 1,305 in the homes, and paid the astonishing number of 6,153 visits. Her district reaches from Point Crewe on the West to Lord's Cove on the East, a distance of eighteen miles. She answers many calls, also, which are long distances from her Centre, going as far as St. Lawrence. This would not be possible but for the motor car given to Nurse Cherry by an American gentleman following the reports of her work during the week of the tidal wave. This is Nurse Cherry's second term with us, her third year. She has made many friends and done much splendid work in that time.*

After the rebuilding operations were underway in the winter of 1929, Nurse Cherry went to St. John's for a vacation. There she received many accolades, including a cheque for $250 from Dr. Mosdell on behalf of the Government of Newfoundland. In sending the cheque to Nurse Cherry, Mosdell wrote, "The whole Government feel that services such as yours should be signally and at the same time practically recognized." Nurse Cherry was also awarded an engraved silver clock from the Nonia executive presented by Lady Middleton at a reception at Government House, the home of the governor.

During the summer of 1930 Nurse Cherry went home to England for a three month holiday. Her local committee back in Lamaline invited her to return and she assured them she would. In fact, she spent many years in Newfoundland, serving as district nurse in Heart's Delight, and ending her career at the Markland Cottage Hospital, where she supervised a staff of nine. Mary Harris, who still lives in nearby Whitbourne, worked with Nurse Cherry as a food supervisor and housekeeper. Mrs. Harris remembers a large silver tray that the people of Lamaline had given to Dorothy after the tidal wave.

Although the two women liked each other, Mary describes Dorothy as a very private person. Indeed, an interesting postscript to the story of this enigmatic hero concerns her life in England prior to her arrival in Newfoundland. Despite the fact that almost all the newspaper accounts and most Nonia records refer to the nurse as Miss Cherry, Dorothy was a widow when she sailed across the Atlantic. Her husband may have been a soldier, as is implied in the preceding text.

In addition, Nurse Cherry seems to have had a daughter who would also have died young. Little information about Dorothy's family is available (thus, I have had to make up a Christian name for her husband on page 95); according to our sources, she rarely spoke of her past or of home. Perhaps her work in Newfoundland served as a refuge of sorts for her:

> *I have been here for some time and have settled in with a garden, profusion of flowers and it seems like home. Markland Hospital is a very pretty one, for it is set back in a wooded land and has nicely kept flower beds. The hospital is built in the style of a bungalow and the rooms are painted in pastel shades. It has accommodation for 17 patients but there are times when beds have to be found for 27.*

In 1947, Nurse Cherry was made a Member of the British Empire for her long years of nursing service in Newfoundland.

I am uncertain which unheralded local men accompanied Nurse Cherry on her post-*tsunami* journey to the stricken communities. From the list of Lamaline residents, I chose Thomas Foote and Albert King, both young, relatively unencumbered, and not too badly affected by the tidal wave. The names of the local members of the relief communities, however, are from the historical record.

Prime Minister Richard Squires was in his second administration during the sad events of 1929. He was exonerated of charges (unrelated) of corruption during this term in an enquiry conducted by Governor Middleton (the same thing had happened during his first term). But the Great Depression and a crippling war debt caught up with the tiny country of Newfoundland and on April 5, 1932, ten thousand city residents rioted outside the Legislature—Squires, in disguise, barely escaped. The House was dissolved two months later and Squires' Liberals lost the election. Squires spent most of his time on his farm on the outskirts of the city and died in 1940 at the age of sixty.

From Part Three, Magistrate Malcolm Hollett later enjoyed a career in politics. He was elected to the National Convention, formed to debate Newfoundland's post-war future at a time when the map of the world was being redrawn. Hollett favoured Responsible Government (roughly, independence) rather than Confederation with Canada. This battle was lost—fifty-two percent to forty-eight percent on a second referendum—but Hollett was elected to the House of Assembly in 1952 and became leader of the Progressive Conservative party the following year. In this capacity, he was leader of the opposition against Premier Joseph Smallwood, holding the position for several years. Hollett's political career ended after ten years in the Canadian Senate.

Captain Dalton is the real name of the man who skippered the *Meigle*, the relief ship sent out by Squires' government. However, so little information was available on him—his first name even seems to be lost to history—that I invented virtually everything else about him. The historical record shows that the relief team of the *Meigle* responded quickly and generously to the dire needs of the people they encountered on their south coast trip; in addition, Dr. Mosdell had written that the captain had been particularly valuable to the relief team. Thus, I envisioned Dalton as a kind and generous man.

The *Meigle* was in the passenger and cargo trade until the early 1930s. In 1932, at the height of the Great Depression, the ship became an auxiliary jail when the penitentiary in St. John's turned out to be too small to hold the thousands of unemployed people who rioted over inadequate government relief. For eight months, the *Meigle* sat in the capital's harbour, known as "the prison afloat," fully staffed with prison personnel. It later returned to more conventional seagoing duties. Finally, after surviving several wartime close calls, in the summer of 1947, the *Meigle* was wrecked at Marines Cove, losing her cargo of live-stock, hens, and pigs. Her crew, however, survived.

Back on the Burin Peninsula, the body of fifteen-year-old Gertrude Fudge of Port au Bras was finally found in July, 1930 entangled in wreckage in the harbour bottom. Gertrude had drowned with her mother, Jessie, and two sisters, Harriet and Hannah, when the waves hauled their house out to sea; the other bodies had been found shortly after the tidal wave. The people of Port au Bras held a church service to remember the victims of the tidal wave on the sixty-fifth anniversary of the disaster ten years ago.

Magistrate Hollett decided to make special arrangements for the widow Lydia Hillier of Point au Gaul as her family had lost their breadwinner and their situation was unique. These arrange-ments are explained in Appendix Five.

Tidal wave victims were not compensated for lost winter pro-visions or their salted fish. Most of the monies paid were for house repairs, lost boats and the like. Not all gear was eligible for compensation. Anecdotally, at least, there is some evidence that many survivors were unhappy with the financial assistance ren-dered. While that is a topic for another book, perhaps, interested readers are referred to *Tidal Wave*, by Garry Cranford.

This book does not pretend to introduce all the heroes of the fall and winter of 1929. Many are already forgotten to history, but one received a standing ovation at the 2004 Symposium of the Newfoundland Historical Society held in St. John's. She is Margaret Giovannini, who lived in St. Lawrence at the time of the *tsunami*, employed as a nurse. According to the Society's Spring

2004 Newsletter, Giovannini's parish priest wrote of her actions at the time:

> *The nurse, scantily clad and wearing house slippers (all her belongings being lost) went from house to house, tending the sick and injured, quelling fears and restoring confidence. She attempted to travel, but roads were blocked by boulders and wreckage. She secured a horse and rode it until it dropped, then she continued on foot. Soaked, chilled to the marrow, she continued her work of mercy all night and part of the next day.*

Meanwhile, as noted in the Society newsletter, Giovannini's summation to headquarters read simply: "Well, but busy."

APPENDIX ONE

St. John's, November 22, 1929
Daily News Editorial

WHEN OUR HEADS ARE BOWED

Recovered from the somewhat unique and rather alarming earth shock of Monday the matter had become with most people, one to joke about, since the occurrence seemed to have passed off without any untoward incident; when suddenly the country was plunged from light levity into a realization that gaunt tragedy of unusual proportions had been enacted close at home. The very genuine expression of sympathy on every lip yesterday, when shortly after noon the first reports of the disastrous effects of the tidal wave on the Burin Peninsula came in, gave a very practical evidence of the way in which that tragedy and distress had touched every heart.

Recovered from the first alarm of the five o'clock earth shock we can picture the inhabitants of these houses gathered around the fire. Supper things had been cleared away. Mother is busy with her knitting or household mending. Children are studying their household lessons. Suddenly, without warning, there is a roar of waters. Louder than that of the ordinary waves on the shore, it breaks on their ears, and then, with a shuddering crash, a fifteen foot wall of water beats on their frail dwelling , pouring in through door and window and carrying back in its undertow, home and mother and children!

The catastrophes of seafaring life we can understand. As a seafaring people we have matched our lives and wits against an old ocean. In the pursuit of their calling as

213

sailors and fishermen, our men dare the ocean's moods; but that in well-found craft where the odds are evenly matched. But in this case women and children and aged people housed in dwellings that had sheltered generations, and proof against winter's blasts and ocean's sprays, were suddenly engulfed and defenceless life obliterated. Never, perhaps, has such a tragedy been enacted in Newfoundland. Certainly never before has an earthquake laid its seafaring finger across our peaceful community.

The loss of property has been very heavy. Stocks of provisions, and fuel accumulated for the winter have been washed away and homes rendered uninhabitable for the present at least. That can be replaced in time; but the lives lost cannot be recalled. We can only mourn and give our deep sympathy to friends and relatives who have been bereaved.

The Government has been ready in action and the rapid dispatch of the relief ship was well engineered and carried out. The *Daily News* has nothing but approval for the prompt response made to the urgent necessities of the unfortunate sufferers in the dispatch of the *Meigle* last night.

APPENDIX TWO

Sympathy Message from Abroad
as it appeared in the *Evening Telegram*, Dec. 16, 1929

Sympathy from the Bishop of London
Bishop's Court, St. John's
13 December, 1929

The Editor *Evening Telegram*

Dear Sir,—The note of sympathy from the Right Hon.
And Right Rev. The Lord Bishop of London, a copy of
which I enclose, will be read not only with great interest
but with deep appreciation by residents in the stricken
parts of the Burin District and by our citizens generally.

Yours very truly,
WILLIAM NEWFOUNDLAND

***

Fulham Palace,

St. Andrew's Day, 1929

Dear Bishop,—I want to send you my deep sympathy
and that of my Diocese with you all in the great misfor-
tune which has occurred in Newfoundland in conse-
quence of the great tidal wave.

I fear that it has worked great havoc among some of
the finest of your people and I would like them to know
how deeply we sympathize with them in London.

215

Maura Hanrahan

If any Fund is being raised to help them I am sure we shall support it to the best of our power.

Yours very sincerely,

A.F. LONDON

APPENDIX THREE

Letter to Local Committee from Relief Expedition

On Board Relief Ship "Meigle",
November 23, 1929.

Mr. C.C. Pittman, J.P.,
Chairman Relief Committee,
For Earthquake Sufferers.

Dear Sir:

Having been given full powers by His Majesty's Government to deal with such relief measures as are required in connection with the recent disaster to various settlements through earthquake shock and tidal wave destruction, we hereby delegate to you the authority to deal with conditions in your district as circumstances may show to be necessary.

You are to act as chairman of the committee which will arrange and supervise the necessary relief measures in the section from Lord's Cove to High Beach, inclusive. Your committee consists of: C.C. Pittman, J.P., Chairman, John Foote, J.P., Rev. Fr. Sullivan, Rev. Mr. Spurrell, Messrs Lewis Crews, John W. Hillier, Edward Cake and John Haley.

Relief supplies for your section are at your disposal to be distributed as you and your committee see fit. You are, further, to take care of clothing supplies, of housing conditions, of fuel and other conditions and to handle these matters as you see fit under all the circumstances, being hereby invested with whatever powers are necessary to enforce your decisions in connection with the various undertakings concerned.

It is not possible to give your duties or to state your powers in detail, but you are generally to undertake and do such things as may from time to time appear to be necessary from the standpoint of relief or to facilitate such relief measures, until you are further advised by the Government of Newfoundland.

The Government are particularly concerned to ascertain the full extent of the damage in your section. You will, therefore, arrange to have a thorough survey made as expeditiously as possible, employing whatever means or agencies are necessary for this purpose and using forms supplied you by us.

We have the honour to be,
Sir,
Your obedient servants
(SGD.)
H.B.C. Lake
H.M. Mosdell
Alex Campbell
P.T. Fudge

APPENDIX FOUR

Letter from Magistrate Hollett to Captain Davis, *Ianthe* (note: Davis was one of the schooner captains commissioned to assist with the relief operations)

Earthquake Relief Committee
Of the Government of Newfoundland

Hon. President: Hon. Sir R.A. Squires, K.C.M.G., M.H.A., Prime Minister
Hon. Chairman: H.B.C. Lake, Esq., M.H.A., Minister of Marine and Fisheries
Hon. Corresponding Secretary: Hon. H.M. Mosdell, M.B., M.H.A., Chairman Nfld. Board of Health
Hon. Members: Hon. A. Barnes, Paed. D., B.Sc., Colonial Secretary
Hon. Alex Campbell, M.D., F.R.C.S. (E), M.H.A.
Malcolm Hollett, Esq.,, B.A. (Oxon), S.M.

Sudbury Building
St. John's, Newfoundland

Burin North
June 14, 1930

Captain Davis
Schooner *Ianthe*
Burin.

Dear Capt. Davis:

I am in receipt of a telegram from Mr. Horwood, Chairman of the South Coast Disaster Fund Committee,

219

Maura Hanrahan

asking me to instruct you to return to St. John's on completion on this trip. You will therefore act accordingly.

I must take this opportunity of thanking you for the very able manner in which you have discharged your duties in taking around to the various harbours and coves the large amounts of materials which the Committee has placed in your charge. You have brought us one load of lumber from St. John's and seven trips of round timber and various quantities of lumber and dories on these eight trips and I consider that you have done wonderful work. For example: On this last trip of the *Ianthe* I have asked you to unload material at eight different places, to wit; High Beach, Lamaline, Point au Gaul, Taylor's Bay, Lord's Cove, Lawn, Corbin and Burin and I have received word from Mr. Foote to state that you have called at each place and discharged the requisite amount of lumber and timber and it has been done very expeditiously.

We all quite realize the difficulty and danger to your ship in discharging at places up the Coast which are situated on a wild shore.

Please accept my thanks and the thanks of the Committee for the energy which you have put into this work.

With kindest regards,
Yours faithfully,
M. Hollett

APPENDIX FIVE

Letter from Magistrate Hollett to South Coast Disaster Committee

Earthquake Relief Committee
Of the Government of Newfoundland

Hon. President: Hon. Sir R.A. Squires, K.C.M.G., M.H.A., Prime Minister
Hon. Chairman: H.B.C. Lake, Esq., M.H.A., Minister of Marine and Fisheries
Hon. Corresponding Secretary: Hon. H.M. Mosdell, M.B., M.H.A., Chairman Nfld. Board of Health
Hon. Members: Hon. A. Barnes, Paed. D., B.Sc., Colonial Secretary
Hon. Alex Campbell, M.D., F.R.C.S. (E), M.H.A.
Malcolm Hollett, Esq.,, B.A. (Oxon), S.M.

Sudbury Building
St. John's, Newfoundland

Burin North
August 15, 1930

R.F. Horwood, Esq.
Chairman, S.C.D.F. Committee
St. John's

Dear Mr. Horwood:

On my last trip up the coast I have come across one or two other claims which I would like to have put in the same class as those others concerning which I have written you and where a cash payment seems to be the correct method.

(1) David Collins of Lamaline Meadow. This man is 83 and crippled and naturally unable to build again his stage which he lost and which he assures me has turned him in $20.00 per year for the last few years. The Stage was 18 x 14 x 8, and he hired it out for several years. He also lost $30.00 worth of clothing and considerable fencing. So far he has taken nothing and I should like to recommend a cash payment of $150.00 in full settlement of his claim which I know would perfectly satisfy the old man.

(2) Edwin King, of Lamaline East, was assessed $170.00 and I understand has so far taken material to amount of $22.50. This man has been sick for five years and has not earned anything, and I know he can never again earn or even get out around, much less build. We should make a satisfied claimant by a cash payment of $150.00 to him also, and I should like to recommend it as a fair and just settlement in this case.

(3) Claim #44. David Strang, Lawn, was assessed $742.00 and I find this claim not only includes David Strang's loss but also that of his adopted son, Peter Quirk. Quirk has taken his share of the assessment, leaving some $300.00 worth still due the claimant David Strang, who has been bedridden these seven years, and who owned the dwelling house, stage and one of the stores. He assures me and I quite believe him, that he can do nothing with material and I would recommend a cash payment of $200.00 be made to settle his claim.

(4) I have already mentioned the case of Mrs. Thos. G. Hillier [author's note: this is Lydia Hillier] of Point aux Gauls [sic] whose husband was drowned. In this connection I would say that her stepson, Harold William,

who gave in the losses of fishing gear and premises etc has been fixed up O.K, but so far no arrangement has been made in a compensation to Mrs. Hillier.

Mrs. Hillier was left with a step-daughter aged 20, a daughter aged 11, and two sons, one 2 years of age and the other an infant born shortly after the husband's death [author's note: this baby was born partially blind]. I am not in a position to know the personal circumstances of Mrs. Hillier but suspect they are not very good as I know Mr. Hillier carried no insurance on account of some heart trouble. There is too I think some little friction between the son Harold William and his step-mother. I would suggest therefore that an arrangement be made whereby the property and fishing gear be left with Harold William and his sister Georgina, and Mrs. Thos. Hillier be made a separate allowance for herself and her children.

As Thomas Hillier was the only bread-winner who lost his life in the Tidal Wave, and as he has left rather a helpless family I beg to suggest that the sum of $3000.00 be set aside in Trust for Mrs. Hillier and her children and that she be paid $25.00 per month out of this sum until the whole be expended. I feel sure this arrangement will meet the needs of the case fairly well, having regard to it's [sic] nature, and the aim of the Funds.

I should be glad to have settlements of these and the other cases which I wrote you about previously, fixed at your earliest convenience either along the lines I have suggested or otherwise as the Committee deem fit.

Yours faithfully,

M. Hollett

APPENDIX SIX

Newfoundland Board of Health
St. John's, Nfld.
South Coast Disaster Summary

1. Extent of coastline affected – 60 miles.

2. Population affected – 10,000.

3. Lives lost – 27, at the following places and to the following extent: Port au Bras, 7; Kelly's Cove, 2; Lord's Cove, 4; Taylor's Bay, 5; Point au Gaul, 8; Allan's Island, 1.

4. Property losses, approximately one million dollars.

5. Industrial effects – boats, fishing gear, supplies and other equipment of fifty per cent of the wage-earners destroyed.

6. Commercial effects – supplying merchants at half a dozen of the larger fishing communities stripped of property and goods rendering it impossible for them to continue in the trade.

In addition to the above, a thorough inspection was made of all settlements visited in the stricken area and many cases of a chronic nature were treated or prescribed for.

Staff—
Dr. L. Paterson,
Dr. C.F. Blackler
Dr. J.B. Murphy
District Nurse D. Cherry
Nurses Jackman, Hampton, Fitzgerald, Rendell

APPENDIX SEVEN

Value of Donations to South Coast Disaster Committee

In-kind gifts: $25,000 value

St. John's: $102,306.23
Rest of Newfoundland: $87,201.38
United States: $8691.57
England: $7440.37
Canada: $36,768.31
Special (amount from Newfoundland, representing funds from Britain, the U.S., and Canada): $7684.28
Interest earned: $4939.60
Sundry refunds: $1896.81, $6836.41
TOTAL: $256,928.55

Note that this sum does not include the goods that were sent with the *Meigle* and the *Daisy* on their early relief voyages or the lumber, clothing, etc. that was sent directly from private firms and communities around the country.

Note also that the Committee did not reimburse people for foodstuffs lost to the *tsunami*.

Sources consulted for *Tsunami*

CORRESPONDENCE AT THE TIME OF THE TIDAL WAVE

Bartlett, George A., Letter to R.A. Squires, Prime Minister, Nov. 20, 1929.

Earthquake Relief Committee of the Government of Newfoundland. Correspondence, 1930.

Ernest Cheeseman, Port au Bras, Letter to John Cheeseman, Nov. 20, 1929.

Hollett, Magistrate M., Correspondence to Prime Minister Squires—various letters and telegraphs, 1929.

Macpherson, Dr. Cluny, Letters to Dr. H.M. Mosdell, Nov. 27 and Dec. 9, 1929.

Mosdell, Dr. H.M., Letters and telegraphs to Hon. Dr. Barnes, Nov. 22, Nov. 27, and Nov. 29, 1929.

Mosdell, Dr. H.M., Letter to Nurse D. Cherry, Jan. 14, 1930.

Mosdell, Dr. H.M., Letter to Dr. Cluny Macpherson, Dec. 6, 1929.

REPORTS FROM THE ERA

Board of Health for the Colony, St. John's, Newfoundland (n.d.) List of Lives Lost in Earthquake Disaster.

Dee, J.H. (1929) Report by Inspector J.H. Dee on Disaster of Night of 18th November on the Coast from Lamaline, Inclusive. Submitted to M. Hollett.

Author Unknown (1929) Voyage of relief Ship *Meigle*—To Scene of Tidal Wave Disaster, Lamaline to Rock Harbour, Districts Burin East and West.

Hollett, M. (1929) Report on Damages, Rock Harbour.

Hollett, M. (1929) Report on Damages by Tidal Wave between Lamaline and Rock Harbour.

Newfoundland Board of Health, (1929) Southwest Coast Disaster Summary. St. John's, Newfoundland.

Newfoundland Outport Nursing Industrial Association (Nonia) (Sept. 30, 1932) Eighth Annual Report, delivered at Nonia Headquarters in St. John's.

Paterson, L., M.D. (1929) List of injured attended by medical staff of *Meigle*.

South Coast Disaster Committee, (July, 1931) Report of the South Coast Disaster Committee. St. John's, Newfoundland.

INTERVIEWS CONDUCTED FOR THIS BOOK

Isabel Gibbons Bragg, St. John's.

Margaret Rennie Saint, Fox Cove.

Elizabeth (Bessie) Hennebury Walsh, Lord's Cove.

Mary Harris, Whitbourne.

CORRESPONDENCE RECEIVED BY FLANKER PRESS

•Sam Adams of London, Ontario, originally of Great Burin.

•Nellie Andrews, Winterland, Newfoundland, originally of Springdale, Newfoundland.

•Anna Tarrant Contois of Barefoot Bay, Florida, originally of Lawn.

•Mary Kehoe Dasting of Cape Coral, Florida, originally of Red Head Cove, Conception Bay, Newfoundland.

•Frederick Davies, Carbonear, Conception Bay, Newfoundland.

•Cyril Fleming of Mississauga, Ontario.

•Marie Herlidan, originally from Lord's Cove.

•Austin Murphy of Toronto, originally from Lawn.

•Aiden O'Brien of Brooklyn, New York, originally of Cape Broyle, Newfoundland.

•Captain Ernest Pike of Summerside, Prince Edward Island, originally from Burin Bay Arm.

•Caroline Hillier Skinner-Hickman of Mississauga, Ontario, originally from Point au Gaul.

•Albert Taylor of Guelph, Ontario, originally from Jamestown, Bonavista Bay, Newfoundland.

OTHER ARCHIVAL MATERIAL

Newfoundland Outport Nursing Industrial Association (Nonia) Collection—various materials, Centre for Newfoundland Studies Archives, Queen Elizabeth II Library, Memorial University of Newfoundland, St. John's, Newfoundland.

PUBLISHED SOURCES

Author Unknown. (2004) "Devotion to Duty of the Highest Order." *Newfoundland Historical Society Newsletter*. Spring 2004: 3.

Brown, Cassie. (1962?) "Earthquake and Tidal Wave: The Hillier Story." *The St. John's Woman Magazine.*

Cranford, Garry. (2000) *Tidal Wave: A List of Victims and Survivors—Newfoundland, 1929.* St. John's, Newfoundland: Flanker Press.

Cranford, Garry. (1999) "Tidal Wave: Adrift in A House— Pearl Hatfield." In *Not Too Long Ago,* 45-46. St. John's, Newfoundland: Seniors Resource Centre.

Cranford, Garry. (1999) "Tidal Wave: On Great Burin Island—Louise Hollett." In *Not Too Long Ago,* 47-49. St. John's, Newfoundland: Seniors Resource Centre.

Cranford, Garry. (1999) "Tidal Wave: At Lord's Cove— Mary McKenna." In *Not Too Long Ago,* 50-51. St. John's, Newfoundland: Seniors Resource Centre.

Cranford, Garry. (1999) "Tidal Wave: My Experience— Eloise Morris." In *Not Too Long Ago,* 52-53. St. John's, Newfoundland: Seniors Resource Centre.

Cranford, Garry. (1999) "Tidal Wave: Kelly's Cove— Marion Moulton." In *Not Too Long Ago,* 54-55. St. John's, Newfoundland: Seniors Resource Centre.

Daily News. (1929-1930) Various articles and editorials.

Decks Awash. (1980-82) Various articles.

Encyclopedia of Newfoundland and Labrador. (1981-1994) Various editions and entries.

Evening Telegram. (1929-1930) Various articles and editorials.

Western Star. (1929-1930) Various articles and editorials.

Acknowledgements

My thanks go to Garry Cranford, whose initial research served as the foundation for this book. In addition, Garry's fine compilation book, *Tidal Wave: A List of Victims and Survivors, Newfoundland, 1929* provided a great deal of the information concerning material losses and loss of life that is contained in this book. In turn, researcher Vera McDonald did much of the work that made Garry's original book possible.

As always, the staff of the Centre for Newfoundland Studies and Archives at Memorial University's QEII Library made my own research much easier with their helpfulness and expertise. The City of Bolton, England kindly forwarded material. The City of St. John's awarded me a grant to partially fund this project, which I greatly appreciate. Thanks to Janice Cheeseman, Margie and Gladys Bonnell, and Harold and Grace Hollett for their assistance and generosity with photographs for *Tsunami*.

Any errors that occur are regrettable and are mine.

I would also like to thank the entire staff of Flanker Press: Margo, Jerry, Brian, Laura, and Bob, who are dedicated, knowledgeable, and great to work with.

Readers who bought *The Doryman* (Flanker, 2003) provided a big incentive to produce this book, especially those older readers on the Burin Peninsula, who remembered the August Gale of 1935 and those younger readers who want more of their own history. The preservation of the memories of those who died in the 1929 tidal wave, in this, the seventy-fifth anniversary year of the disaster, were another reason to write this book.

I am grateful to my husband, Paul Butler, for enthusiasm, support, and sharp editing. Finally, much thanks to Vanessa.